Easy Oracle PL/SQL
Get Started Fast with Working PL/SQL Code Examples

John Garmany

This book is dedicated to the most important person in my life, my wife.
– John Garmany

Easy Oracle PL/SQL
Get Started Fast with Working PL/SQL Code Examples

By John Garmany

Copyright © 2006 by Rampant TechPress. All rights reserved.

Printed in the United States of America.

Published by: Rampant TechPress, Kittrell, NC, USA

Editors: John Lavender and Janet Burleson

Production Editor: Teri Wade

Production Manager: Linda Webb

Cover Design: Bryan Hoff

Illustrations: Mike Reed

Printing History:

March 2006 for First Edition

ISBN: 0-9759135-7-3

Library of Congress Control Number: 2005928019

Table of Contents

Using the Online Code Depot

Purchase of this book provides complete access to the online code depot that contains the sample code scripts. All of the code depot scripts in this book are located at the following URL:

rampant.cc/easy_plsql.htm

All of the code scripts in this book are available for download in zip format, ready to load and use. If technical assistance is needed with downloading or accessing the scripts, please contact Rampant TechPress at info@rampant.cc.

Are you WISE?

Get the premier Oracle tuning tool. The Workload Interface Statistical Engine for Oracle provides unparallel capability for time-series Oracle tuning, unavailable nowhere else.

WISE supplements Oracle Enterprise Manager and it can quickly plot and spot performance signatures to allow you to see hidden trends, fast.

WISE interfaces with STATSPACK or AWR to provide unprecedented proactive tuning insights. Best of all, it is only $9.95. Get WISE download Now!

www.wise-oracle.com

Conventions Used in this Book

It is critical for any technical publication to follow rigorous standards and employ consistent punctuation conventions to make the text easy to read.

However, this is not an easy task. Within Oracle there are many types of notation that can confuse a reader. Some Oracle utilities such as STATSPACK and TKPROF are always spelled in CAPITAL letters, while Oracle parameters and procedures have varying naming conventions in the Oracle documentation. It is also important to remember that many Oracle commands are case sensitive, and are always left in their original executable form, and never altered with italics or capitalization.

Hence, all Rampant TechPress books follow these conventions:

Parameters - All Oracle parameters will be *lowercase italics*. Exceptions to this rule are parameter arguments that are commonly capitalized (KEEP pool, TKPROF), these will be left in ALL CAPS.

Variables - All PL/SQL program variables and arguments will also remain in *lowercase italics* (*dbms_job, dbms_utility*).

Tables & dictionary objects – All data dictionary objects are referenced in *lowercase italics* (*dba_indexes, v$sql*). This includes all *v$* and *x$* views (*x$kcbcbh, v$parameter*) and dictionary views (*dba_tables, user_indexes*).

SQL - All SQL is formatted for easy use in the code depot. The main SQL terms (select, from, where, group by, order by, having) will always appear on a separate line.

Programs & Products - All products and programs that are known to the author are capitalized according to the vendor specifications (IBM, DBXray, etc). All names known by

---

Rampant TechPress to be trademark names appear in this text as initial caps. References to UNIX are always made in uppercase.

Acknowledgements

This type of highly technical reference book requires the dedicated efforts of many people. Even though we are the authors, our work ends when we deliver the content.

After each chapter is delivered, several Oracle DBAs carefully review and correct the technical content. After the technical review, experienced copy editors polish the grammar and syntax.

The finished work is then reviewed as page proofs and turned over to the production manager, who arranges the creation of the online code depot and manages the cover art, printing distribution, and warehousing.

In short, the authors play a small role in the development of this book, and we need to thank and acknowledge everyone who helped bring this book to fruition:

John Lavender, for the production management, including the coordination of the cover art, page proofing, printing, and distribution.

Teri Wade, for her help in the production of the page proofs.

Bryan Hoff, for his exceptional cover design and graphics.

Janet Burleson, for her assistance with the web site, and for creating the code depot and the online shopping cart for this book.

Linda Webb, for her expert page-proofing services.

Don Burleson, for his expert technical review of the content.

With my sincerest thanks,

John Garmany

Preface

This book is a companion to my Easy Oracle SQL book. It is not so much a sequel as a continuation. I have been working with Oracle databases and SQL for many years but it was not until I started teaching SQL and PL/SQL that I really started to learn it. There is nothing like a student question to put you on the spot.

When Oracle put Java in the database, many of my friends decided that they should focus on Java and quit using PL/SQL. To this day, they are still better PL/SQL developers than Java developers. As you learn PL/SQL, you will realize the same thing they realized, that PL/SQL is unique in its ability to effectively and efficiently operate on the data stored in an Oracle database.

In fact, Java (and other language) programmers are seeing the benefit of encapsulating all an application SQL in PL/SQL procedures and functions, and then calling these procedures and functions rather than executing the SQL from the application.

This book will introduce you to the power and capability of Oracle's Procedural Language extensions to Structured Query Language or PL/SQL. One important note is that PL/SQL is an extension to SQL. You must have a good working understanding of SQL before starting PL/SQL. This book assumes you have that knowledge. If you are a little rusty on your SQL, you might want to look at the book Easy Oracle SQL as a refresher. Chapter 1 orients you to the Oracle database, SQL*Plus and the PUBS training database schema. From that point on, it is pure PL/SQL.

PL/SQL provides all the basic programming structures, from IF/THEN statements to a variety of LOOPs. Unlike any other programming language (other than Java) PL/SQL executes in the Oracle database. PL/SQL is designed to efficiently interact with the Oracle database and take advantage of the power of the database server. If you program in Java or C++, the structures will be familiar with some database centric adjustments. Variable data types and structures are implemented to interact with the database. Collections are limited because a programmer does not have to work exclusively in memory; there is a powerful database system providing data persistence. Programmers tend to pickup PL/SQL quickly.

Unlike SQL, PL/SQL is Oracle centric. No other database system will execute PL/SQL. To run the examples you will need an Oracle database. The examples in this book have been run on Oracle9i, Oracle10g and the new free OracleXE.

If you do not have an Oracle database to practice, I suggest going to the Oracle technology Network web page (otn.oracle.com) and downloading the OracleXE database. This free database has a complete implementation of the SQL and PL/SQL engines. I have run all the code in the code depot through the XE database without an issue.

Finally, one of my biggest complaints is computer books that tell you to do something, but not how to do it. Sometimes they provide a simple example that is no help in solving your real work problem. I have made an attempt to include as many examples as possible in this book.

Feedback is always welcome regarding how to improve this book, and you are encouraged to contact me with suggestions at john.garmany@dba-oracle.com.

Introduction to PL/SQL CHAPTER

1

Introduction to PL/SQL

Databases have been in use long before the personal computer arrived on the scene. IBM developed the Structured Query Language standard (dubbed SQL, and pronounced "See-Quel") over 30 years ago as a way to retrieve data from their new "relational" database. A decade later, Oracle released the first commercial relational database that used SQL, and SQL has become the de-facto query language for the vast majority of popular database products.

Even though SQL is the standard language for interacting with any modern database, it does not mean that SQL is without limitations. If we want to retrieve a set of records from the database and modify them according to a set of rules, (updating some and returning to the calling program others), we can't do this with a single SQL call to the database. Complex processing requires the ability to compare values (often called Boolean logic) and implement programmatic flow control. In other words, some type of programming language was required to process the returned rows and implement the program rules. To achieve this capability, Oracle introduced the Procedural Language extensions to the Structured Query Language or PL/SQL.

Oracle PL/SQL was based on the ADA programming language which was developed by the Department of Defense to be used on mission critical systems. Although not a "sexy" language like Java or C, ADA is still being develop and used for applications

---

such as aircraft control systems. ADA is a highly structured, strongly typed programming language that uses natural language constructs to make it easy to understand. The PL/SQL language inherited these attributes making PL/SQL easier to read and maintain than more cryptic languages such as C. For example, below are two loops, one in PL/SQL and the other in a programming language called C.

```
for x in v_start..v_finish --PL/SQL
loop
   v_int := v_int +1;
end loop;
```

As opposed to

```
for (x = str; x< fin; x++) {i++}   --C
```

As we see, the PL/SQL statement is more verbose but also easier to understand.

PL/SQL is also portable within the Oracle database family and runs on all supported Oracle platforms including Oracle10g grid database. Even more important is platform independence, where programs developed in PL/SQL on a Windows Oracle database will load and run in a UNIX Oracle database. With each release of the Oracle database, Oracle Corporation enhances the capabilities and performance of PL/SQL. Remember, PL/SQL is an Oracle only product, and no other database management system will run PL/SQL.

Unlike other languages that execute externally, PL/SQL executes inside the database. This means that you can take advantage of PL/SQL's exceptional ability to manipulate data in the database without paying the network penalty of retrieving the data out of the database and them updating it back to the database. Because PL/SQL runs inside the database it takes advantage of the capabilities and capacity of the database server.

Traditionally, PL/SQL has been a compiled/interpreted language similar to Java. When PL/SQL code is loaded into the database it is compiled into an intermediate form, similar to the way Java is compiled into byte-code. This intermediate code is portable across Oracle databases. Later versions of Oracle (Oracle9i and 10g) will compile PL/SQL into native code for over 60 hardware platforms. This natively compiled code runs more efficiently, but it loses the ability to move to other Oracle databases without recompiling.

Lastly, placing the code that interacts with the database in PL/SQL makes better use of the database resources. PL/SQL packages are loaded as a package so as your program calls for data, the procedures and functions are already in cached memory. Using PL/SQL will also result in your application using bind variables. The only way not to use bind variables in PL/SQL is to implement dynamic SQL (discussed in Chapter 5). The Database Administrator (DBA) also benefits when developers place their SQL inside PL/SQL because they have access to the statements for tuning. For example the DBA can tune the SQL (adding hints, reordering the WHERE clause) without impacting the existing application. Placing SQL inside PL/SQL also allows the code to be protected by the recovery capabilities of the Oracle database.

PL/SQL is the most common language for Oracle the world, and developers are realizing the benefits in both application performance and database performance by implementing the database interaction in PL/SQL. There are even websites built entirely using PL/SQL. For example, Oracle's HTML-DB product is installed in the database and consists primarily of PL/SQL packages and Java scripts.

Maximizing your Learning

This book is designed to be a high-level introduction to PL/SQL. There are many advanced capabilities of PL/SQL that exceed the scope of this book, but the good news is that they are all built on the programming foundations covered in this book. To maximize your learning you should work the examples, and all the examples in this book were developed using TextPad, a text application like Windows' notepad. There is no need to use a development environment to learn PL/SQL and in teaching PL/SQL over the years, we have found that development environments such as JDeveloper or Toad tend to confuse the new PL/SQL developer. Once you begin developing application, you will find these tools valuable assets. The examples in this book were tested against Oracle9i and Oracle10g and the new free Oracle XE database.

The examples used in this book use a small training database called PUBS. The following two sections discuss installing the PUBS database and using SQL*Plus. If you started with the book *Easy Oracle SQL*, you already have the PUBS database installed and know how to use SQL*Plus. You may want to jump to the section titled PL/SQL Basic Structures in this chapter. Let's take a closer look at the PUBS database.

The PUBS Database

For the remainder of the book we will create examples that use the PUBS database schema. This database was designed as a teaching tool and is available in the code depot.

🖫 **pubs_db.sql (see code depot)**

The file is a list of Oracle commands that creates and populates the database schema. The commands are discussed in detail in the companion SQL book, *Easy Oracle SQL.*

Installing the PUBS database creates a user called pubs and grants the Role DBA to that user. As such, this script should only be used in a training/test/development environment.

To install the PUBS database you need a running oracle database and we assume that you have already successfully installed the Oracle database. If not, you need to go to otn.oracle.com and download the latest version of the Oracle database. We recommend downloading the new Oracle XE database, which is free and contains the latest version of the PL/SQL engine. All the examples in this book were tested on Oracle9i, Oracle10g and Oracle XE Beta.

1. When the database was created you assigned it a System ID (called a "SID") and OracleXE uses the SID named "XE".

2. Create a practice directory and copy the *pubs_db.sql* file to this practice directory.

3. Start the database.

4. On Windows go to services, right click and start the service OracleService<SID>. Then start the service OracleListener.

5. On Linux/Unix you must set the environmental variables Oracle Home and Oracle SID before starting the database. Substitute the correct information in the example below.

```
$ export ORACLE_HOME=/opt/oracle
$ export ORACLE_SID=mydb
$ sqlplus "/ as sysdba"
SQL> startup
SQL> exit
$ lsnrctl start
```

In both cases we started two programs, the database and the listener. The listener listens on a port (normally port number 1521 but you can change the port) for a connection. When you connect to the database, the listener takes your connection request and creates a server process to perform the actual database work.

6. Open a terminal window and change into the practice directory.

7. On Windows select Start – Run – type cmd and press enter.

8. On Linux right click on the desktop and select terminal.

9. Change to the practice directory

```
C:> cd c:\practice
$ cd practice
```

Code Depot User ID = reader; Password = easysql

All the examples in this book will use SQL*Plus. This is Oracle's command line tool for interacting with the database. We will go into SQL*Plus in much more detail later. Start SQL*Plus as the super user.

```
$ sqlplus "/ as sysdba"
SQL>
```

After starting, SQL*Plus will leave you at the *SQL>* prompt. To load the PUBS database, you will need to run the *pubs_db.sql* script.

```
SQL> @pubs_db.sql
```

This will create the pubs user with a password of pubs, create the tables and load the data. When you are through you will be left as the user pubs. You can verify this with the command below:

```
SQL> show user
PUBS
SQL> exit
```

Use exit to get back to the operating system prompt.

The code depot also contains a PowerPoint slide (*PUBS_DB.ppt*) with the diagram of the PUBS database. The PUBS database details information about publishing books. There is an author table which list authors. Notice that it contains a unique key called the *auth_key* that uniquely identifies each author. The *book* table lists the books. The *store* table list stores that sell the books and the sales table list books sold, by order number, in each store. A publisher also has and *employee* table for the employees who print the books.

You can see the links between each table. Notice the *book_author* table. This is a weak entity needed to eliminate the many-to-many link between the *author* table and the *book* table, representing the fact that an author can write many books and a book can have more than one author. The *book_author* table eliminates that many-to-many link between author and book. The primary key in the *book_author* table is both the *auth_key* and the *book_key* (a multicolumn key).

PL/SQL and SQL*Plus

At this point you should have your Oracle database started and loaded with the PUBS schema and it is now time to move to using PL/SQL. In Oracle, SQL is divided into three basic groups of commands including queries, Data Definition Language (DDL) and Data Manipulation Language (DML).

- **Queries** – We use the SELECT operator to perform data extractions

- **DDL** – Data Definition Language is used to define objects within the database such as creating tables or indexes.

- **DML** – Data Manipulation Language is used to insert, update and delete data in the database.

Remember, PL/SQL is a programming language that is tightly integrated with SQL. It has the ability to retrieve and manipulate data, but also to execute DDL and other PL/SQL code.

PL/SQL runs on the database server, not on the local client machine. Unlike external programs, PL/SQL takes advantage of the power and safety of the Oracle database, its security and protection. By executing on the database server, PL/SQL also avoids the most time consuming part of interacting with the database, the passing of result-sets back-and-forth across the network.

The examples in this book are created using SQL*Plus, the command line interface to the Oracle Database. You may chose to use one of the PL/SQL integrated development environments such as TOAD, PL/SQL Developer or Oracle's new Raptor. For a new developer we recommend using SQL*Plus because it is simple and will keep you from confusing PL/SQL errors and the tool errors. You will find that the first thing a developer needs to do is understand the Oracle and PL/SQL error messages. Remember, a development tool can make error messages harder to understand.

The first step is to start SQL*Plus and connect to the database. In Windows, open a terminal window. In Linux/Unix go to the command line and ensure that the database environment is set. To start SQL*Plus just enter the "sqlplus" command. If the program is not found, make sure the ORACLE_HOME is set in the path.

```
[oracle@appsvr oracle]$ sqlplus
SQL*Plus: Release 10.1.0.2.0 - Production on Thu Jan 20 20:23:44
2005
Copyright (c) 1982, 2004, Oracle.  All rights reserved.
Enter user-name:
```

The example database is called DEVDB. You can start SQL*Plus and log on in one command like below.

```
[oracle@appsvr oracle]$ sqlplus pubs/pubs@devdb
SQL*Plus: Release 10.1.0.2.0 - Production on Thu Jan 20 20:28:11
2005
Copyright (c) 1982, 2004, Oracle.  All rights reserved.
Connected to:
Oracle Database 10g Enterprise Edition Release 10.1.0.2.0 -
Production
With the Partitioning, OLAP and Data Mining options
SQL>
```

The log on format is *username/password@database_service_name*. The database service name is the name of the entry in the *tnsnames.ora* file located in the *$ORACLE_HOME/network/admin/tnsnames.ora*. You may need to get with your DBA to setup the *tnsnames.ora* file. If you are running SQL*Plus on the computer that you installed Oracle on, the installation program created a TNSNAMES entry that matches the database SID, in my case DEVDB.

If there was someone watching you log on and you didn't want them to see the password, do not included it and SQL*Plus will ask for it (and not echo the password to the screen).

```
[oracle@appsvr oracle]$ sqlplus pubs@devdb
SQL*Plus: Release 10.1.0.2.0 - Production on Thu Jan 20 20:29:54
2005
Copyright (c) 1982, 2004, Oracle.  All rights reserved.
Enter password:
Connected to:
Oracle Database 10g Enterprise Edition Release 10.1.0.2.0 -
Production
With the Partitioning, OLAP and Data Mining options
SQL>
```

We recommend that you print a copy of the pubs.ppt slide in the code depot for easy reference. Look at the *author* table on the slide. You can also see what makes up the *author* table by describing it from the SQL*Plus prompt.

```
SQL> desc author

Name                                Null?     Type
--------------------------------    --------  ------------
AUTHOR_KEY                                    VARCHAR2(11)
AUTHOR_LAST_NAME                              VARCHAR2(40)
AUTHOR_FIRST_NAME                             VARCHAR2(20)
AUTHOR_PHONE                                  VARCHAR2(12)
AUTHOR_STREET                                 VARCHAR2(40)
AUTHOR_CITY                                   VARCHAR2(20)
AUTHOR_STATE                                  VARCHAR2(2)
AUTHOR_ZIP                                    VARCHAR2(5)
AUTHOR_CONTRACT_NBR                           NUMBER(5)
```

This command lists the columns and their definitions.

SQL*Plus places each statement including an anonymous PL/SQL block into a buffer. You can edit the SQL*Plus buffer but it is more efficient to create and run scripts (unless you are a "vi" cowboy, the wildly popular UNIX editor) When you enter a SQL statement, SQL*Plus will continue to place it into the buffer until it encounters a semicolon. This tells SQL*Plus to execute the command. In PL/SQL, each line is terminated in a semicolon.

SQL*Plus waits until you enter a forward slash to send the buffer to the database for execution. You can re-execute the previous statement or block by entering a forward slash (/) or by entering RUN. To list the current buffer enter 'L'. When you enter a carriage return without a semicolon, SQL*Plus assumes you are still entering a command and will provide another line. The Windows version of SQL*Plus also has a command history that you can cycle through using the Up/Down arrows.

PL/SQL deals with blocks of code or scripts. You must use a text editor to create the script and then use SQL*Plus to execute it. The easiest way to do this is to use the host command. On Windows, enter "*host notepad <filename>*" at the SQL*Plus prompt to open a text file in notepad. Write/edit the query or PL/SQL block, save and close the file, then execute it with the "*@<filename>*" command. On Windows to re-edit the file, hit the up arrow to bring the host command back, enter and edit the query. In this way you can quickly go from editing to execution and back to editing. Sadly, Linux/Unix will not scroll through previous commands with the arrow keys without using a separate utility.

To get a list of SQL*Plus command type "help index".

```
SQL> help index

Enter Help [topic] for help.

    @              COPY           PAUSE                 SHUTDOWN
    @@             DEFINE         PRINT                 SPOOL
    /              DEL            PROMPT                SQLPLUS
    ACCEPT         DESCRIBE       QUIT                  START
    APPEND         DISCONNECT     RECOVER               STARTUP
    ARCHIVE LOG    EDIT           REMARK                STORE
    ATTRIBUTE      EXECUTE        REPFOOTER             TIMING
    BREAK          EXIT           REPHEADER             TTITLE
    BTITLE         GET            RESERVED WORDS (SQL)  UNDEFINE
    CHANGE         HELP           RESERVED WORDS (PL/SQL) VARIABLE
    CLEAR          HOST           RUN                   WHENEVER
```

For more detail use "help <command>"

```
SQL> help column

    COLUMN
    ------

    Specifies display attributes for a given column, such as:
        - text for the column heading
        - alignment for the column heading
        - format for NUMBER data
        - wrapping of column data
    Also lists the current display attributes for a single column
    or all columns.

    COL[UMN] [{column | expr} [option ...] ]

    where option represents one of the following clauses:
        ALI[AS] alias
        CLE[AR]
        ENTMAP {ON|OFF}
        FOLD_A[FTER]
        FOLD_B[EFORE]
```

```
FOR[MAT] format
HEA[DING] text
JUS[TIFY] {L[EFT] | C[ENTER] | R[IGHT]}
LIKE {expr | alias}
NEWL[INE]
NEW_V[ALUE] variable
NOPRI[NT] | PRI[NT]
NUL[L] text
OLD_V[ALUE] variable
ON|OFF
WRA[PPED] | WOR[D_WRAPPED] | TRU[NCATED]
```

It bears repeating that PL/SQL is tightly coupled to SQL. If you are not comfortable with SQL you will find PL/SQL very difficult. This book uses Oracle's SQL functions throughout the examples. These SQL functions are covered in detail in the companion book *Easy Oracle SQL*.

Exercises

Below is a set of review SQL exercises that will help you determine if additional time with SQL may be needed. All the exercises use the PUBS database. The answers and an example SQL statement for each exercise are located in the code depot.

1. How do you find the table names for the Pubs schema?

2. How do you find all tables that you have access to?

3. What Columns are in the Book table?

4. How many Authors are in the Author table?

5. List Book Titles in Publication Date order.

6. List Authors and their Book Titles.

7. List Store Names and total Books sold.

8. What is the Avg Number of Books Sold in Stores.

9. Which Stores have above average sales?

If you sailed through the exercises you are ready to move on to PL/SQL.

PL/SQL Basic Structure

PL/SQL developers must be good with Blocks

Like the ADA programming language, PL/SQL is based on blocks, and   PL/SQL provides a number of different blocks for different uses. The characteristics of a block include:

- A block begins with a declarative section where variables are defined.

- This is followed by a section containing the procedural statements surrounded by the BEGIN and END key words. Each block must have a BEGIN and END statement, and may optionally include an *exception* section to handle errors. The exception section is covered later in the book.

Here is an example of a simple block:

```
SQL> declare
  2    v_line varchar2(40);
  3  begin
  4    v_line := 'Hello World';
  5    dbms_output.put_line (v_line);
  6  end;
  7  /

Hello World
```

In the example above, the variable *v_line* is defined in the declarative section on line 2. Like SQL statements, each line ends with a semicolon. Once *v_line* is defined, it can be used in the procedural section. First, *v_line* is assigned the literal string 'Hello World' on line 4. Strings are surrounded by single quotes in SQL and PL/SQL. The *v_line* variable is then placed in the output buffer using the procedure *dbms_output.put_line*.

In PL/SQL, the semicolon defines the end of a line of code. To execute the PL/SQL block, use the forward slash "/" on a line by itself as shown on line 7. If you forget the forward slash, SQL*Plus will simply wait for the next line to be entered.

Note: If you execute a PL/SQL script and SQL*Plus returns a number, it probably is an indication that you forgot to place the"/" at the end of your script. SQL*Plus is actually waiting for the next line. Entering a "/" will execute the script.

A PL/SQL block with no name is called an anonymous block. It starts with the *declare* key word to define the declarative section.

```
declare
    …   define variables here
begin
    …   code goes here
exceptions
end;
```

A named block is a procedure or a function. The name portion defines the declarative section so the DECLARE key word is not used.

```
create procedure my_proc
as
    …  define variables here
begin
    …  code goes here
exceptions
end;
```

A procedure can be passed and change variables. A function can be passed variables and must return a variable.

```
create function my_func (v_name varchar2)return number
as
    …  define variables here
begin
    …  code goes here
    return n_jobNum;
end;
```

When variables are passed to a procedure or function they can be IN, OUT or INOUT. An IN variable is passed into the procedure or function and is used, but can not be changed. An OUT variable is passed to the procedure but it can be changed and left in the changed state when the procedure ends.

An INOUT variable is passed to a procedure or function, and it can be used by the block, changed by the block, and left in a "changed" state when the block ends. A function can only be passed an IN variable and must return a variable. If this is confusing, don't worry. When we get to name blocks and provide some examples it will be much clearer.

Displaying PL/SQL Output

Another change with PL/SQL from SQL is that the database does not return the output. PL/SQL code normally will change data, insert values, and so forth, inside the database. It will not normally display results back to the user. To do this we use a procedure called *dbms_output.put_line* to place the results in a buffer that SQL*Plus will retrieve and display. SQL*Plus must be told to retrieve data from this buffer in order to display the results. The SQL*Plus command *"set serveroutput on"* causes SQL*Plus to retrieve and display the buffer.

```
SQL> declare
  2    v_line varchar2(40);
  3  begin
  4    v_line := 'Hello World';
  5    dbms_output.put_line (v_line);
  6  end;
  7  /

PL/SQL procedure successfully completed.

SQL> set serveroutput on
SQL> declare
  2    v_line varchar2(40);
  3  begin
  4    v_line := 'Hello World';
  5    dbms_output.put_line (v_line);
  6  end;
  7  /
Hello World

PL/SQL procedure successfully completed.
```

The first time the script is run, the result was just a notice that the script completed successfully. Once we *set serveroutput on* and rerun the script, the results are shown.

As discussed earlier, this is an anonymous block of PL/SQL code. It is sent to the database, compiled and executed, then SQL*Plus retrieves the results. The script is stored in the SQL*Plus buffer and can be rerun by executing the forward slash.

```
SQL> /
Hello World

PL/SQL procedure successfully completed.
```

The script is not stored in the database as a stored or named procedure is. It must be resent to the database and compiled each time it is executed.

As with SQL statements, SQL*Plus variables can be used to make the PL/SQL script dynamic. Just as with a SQL statement, the variables are local to SQL*Plus and are substituted before the code is sent to the database.

```
SQL> declare
  2     v_line varchar2(40);
  3  begin
  4     v_line := 'Hello &name';
  5     dbms_output.put_line (v_line);
  6  end;
  7  /
Enter value for name: John
old   4:     v_line := 'Hello &name';
new   4:     v_line := 'Hello John';
Hello John

PL/SQL procedure successfully completed
```

The SQL*Plus *accept* command is a more flexible method of embedding dynamic data in the script.

```
SQL> accept v_string prompt "Enter Your First Name: "

Enter Your First Name: Thomas

SQL> declare
  2     v_line varchar2(40):= '&v_string';
  3  begin
  4     v_line := 'Hello '||v_line;
  5     dbms_output.put_line (v_line);
  6  end;
  7  /

old   2:     v_line varchar2(40):= '&v_string';
new   2:     v_line varchar2(40):= 'Thomas';

Hello Thomas

PL/SQL procedure successfully completed.
```

Let's look at this script a little closer. The first line is the SQL*Plus *accept* command to get the SQL*Plus variable *v_string*.

This line must be executed alone, not part of the PL/SQL block. At the prompt the name Thomas was entered. Now the script is run but it is slightly modified from previous examples.

```
SQL> declare
  2    v_line varchar2(40):= '&v_string';
```

The variable *v_line* is declared as a varchar2(40) and is given a default value that equals *v_string*. The PL/SQL assignment operator (:=) is used to assign the value. So *v_line* is a bucket that gets assigned the string 'Thomas'. A developer would read an assignment statement in English as "v_line gets v_string" to indicate the assignment. Let's examine a more complex assignment statement.

```
  4    v_line := 'Hello '||v_line;
```

Line 4 uses the concatenate operator to append 'Hello ' to the front of *v_line* and then assigns it back to the variable *v_line*. The variable *v_line* now contains the string 'Hello Thomas'. Line 5 places the value of *v_line* in the buffer to be retrieved by SQL*Plus.

```
old   2:   v_line varchar2(40):= '&v_string';
new   2:   v_line varchar2(40):= 'Thomas';
```

These two lines demonstrate SQL*Plus's verify function showing us what is substituted before the code is sent to the database for execution. This information can be switched on/off with the verify command

```
SQL> set verify on
SQL> set verify off
```

Code Readability in PL/SQL

Code readability is important when programming. Many times lines can be combined to reduce the size of the code but may make the code less understandable to anyone other than the author. The example shown earlier can in fact be written with only three lines of code.

```
SQL> begin
  2    dbms_output.put_line ('Hello &v_string');
  3  end;
  4  /

Enter value for v_string: John
Hello John
```

White Space and Comments

As with any programming, you want your script to be as readable as possible. Remember, you may be writing the procedure but more than likely someone else will have to update and maintain it.

White space is added to make code more readable. It has no impact on the execution time or efficiency of the code. White space is use only to make the code more readable to humans. In the examples above, the code between the *begin* and *end* key word is indented. This makes the block boundaries easier to see in the code. The two spaces forming the indent exists only to make the code easier to read. Blank lines can also be used to separate sections of code. Blank lines can appear anywhere in the code (except inside a SQL statement).

PL/SQL Code Comments

PL/SQL supports two types of comments. If the commend is only one line, you can use the double hyphen (--) to mark a line as a comment. Multiple lines can be commented by bracketing them with the slash star (/*...*/).

```
SQL> declare
  2    v_line varchar2(40);
  3  begin
  4    -- this is a single line comment
```

```
 5    v_line := 'Hello World';
 6    dbms_output.put_line (v_line);
 7    /*  This is a
 8        multiple line
 9        comment
10    */
11  end;/

Hello World
```

It has become common to document the code by adding comments that explain not only what the procedure (function or block) does but also defines exactly what variables are passed and how they are changed. This "self documented" code is invaluable in assisting someone who has to later maintain the code. Here is a good example.

```
SQL> declare
 2    /*  This anonymous block uses a SQL*Plus
 3        variable as input, appends Hello to
 4        the front and writes it out to the
 5        buffer.
 6
 7        Requirements:
 8        1.  v_string must be defined before
            execution
 9        2.  Must set serveroutput on to retrieve
10            results
11    */
12    v_line varchar2(40):= '&v_string';
13  begin
14    v_line := 'Hello '||v_line;
15    dbms_output.put_line (v_line);
16  end;
17  /

Enter value for v_string: Sammy

old  12:    v_line varchar2(40):= '&v_string';
new  12:    v_line varchar2(40):= 'Sammy';

Hello Sammy
```

Next, let's look at variable declaration and manipulation.

Variable Declaration and Conversion

In the previous examples a variable *v_line* was defined. All variables are defined in the declaration section of the block. Variables are defined in the form:

```
variableName       datatype       := defaultvalue;
```

Below are examples of variables. Variables can be defined as any valid datatype to include user defined datatypes and records.

```
declare
  v_str1    varchar2(80);
  v_str2    varchar2(30) := 'Hello World';
  d_today   date;
  n_sales   number;
  n_order   number(8);
begin
```

A constant is defined the same way a variable is with the key word *constant*.

```
c_standard constant number := 90;
```

Notice that a constant must be assigned a value and the above statement does four things:

- Names the variable *c_standard*

- Defines *c_standard* as a constant

- Defines *c_standard* as a numeric datatype

- Assigns a value of 90 to *c_standard*

With PL/SQL constants, note that a constant value can't be changed unless it is redefined in a subsequent block.

In the examples above our two variables are defined as numbers, and we are now ready to see how to include the precision and scale for a number. As in SQL, PL/SQL supports mathematical operations and has a large library of mathematical functions, covering everything from advanced multivariate statistics to Newtonian Calculus. PL/SQL also supports single-row functions to convert numbers to characters and characters to numbers.

Use Consistent PL/SQL Variable Naming

Lastly, we need to talk about the importance of using consistent naming conventions. You should define the programming style you will use in defining variables and all members of the programming staff should follow it. In the example above, varchars start with "v_", constants "c_", dates "d_" and numbers as "n_". As the programming procedures and functions become larger and more complicated, the ability to identify what a variable is becomes more important. This naming example is rather simplistic and will be used throughout this book.

The following script accepts two numbers. Because they are stored in SQL*Plus variables, they are actually character strings. The *to_number* function is used to convert them from strings to numbers.

```
SQL> accept v_numb1 prompt "Enter the First Number: "
Enter the First Number: 5
SQL> accept v_numb2 prompt "Enter the Second Number: "
Enter the Second Number: 3
SQL> set serveroutput on
SQL> set serveroutput on
SQL> set verify off
SQL> declare
  2    v_out number := 0;
  3  begin
  4    v_out := to_number('&v_numb1') * to_number('&v_numb2');
  5    dbms_output.put_line ('Multiplication: '||to_char(v_out));
  6    v_out := to_number('&v_numb1') / to_number('&v_numb2');
  7    dbms_output.put_line ('Division:       '||to_char(v_out));
  8    v_out := to_number('&v_numb1') + to_number('&v_numb2');
  9    dbms_output.put_line ('Addition:       '||to_char(v_out));
 10    v_out := to_number('&v_numb1') - to_number('&v_numb2');
 11    dbms_output.put_line ('Subtraction:    '||to_char(v_out));
 12  end;
 13  /
```

```
Multiplication: 15
Division:     1.6666666666666666666666666666666666667
Addition:     8
Subtraction:  2
```

The built-in function *to_number* is actually a PL/SQL function provided by Oracle and it is the same single row function used in a SQL statement. It is passed a character variable and returns a number. Internally, Oracle will automatically convert between number and characters without you having to implicitly use a function to convert. The previous example could be re-written without the *to_number* function, like this.

```
SQL> declare
  2     v_out number := 0;
  3  begin
  4     v_out := &v_numb1 * '&v_numb2';
  5     dbms_output.put_line ('Multiplication: '||to_char(v_out));
  6     v_out := '&v_numb1' / &v_numb2;
  7     dbms_output.put_line ('Division:       '||to_char(v_out));
  8     v_out := &v_numb1 + '&v_numb2';
  9     dbms_output.put_line ('Addition:       '||to_char(v_out));
 10     v_out := '&v_numb1' - &v_numb2;
 11     dbms_output.put_line ('Subtraction:    '||to_char(v_out));
 12  end;
 13  /

Multiplication: 15
Division:     1.6666666666666666666666666666666666667
Addition:     8
Subtraction:  2

PL/SQL procedure successfully completed.
```

If the database can determine that a conversion is necessary, it will automatically execute it. Sometimes, for readability, you may want to implicitly convert variables so that others reading the code will know that a conversion it taking place.

When a PL/SQL block contains a SQL statement, that statement can include any function or conversion that a stand alone SQL statement can use to include single-row functions, multi-row functions, grouping, sorting and the special *decode* function.

All the single-row functions can also be used in the PL/SQL block, outside of a SQL statement.

```
v_name := lower(&v_string);
v_str_long := 'Hello Student'||CHR(10)||'Bye';
```

The first example uses the *lower* function to change the SQL*Plus variable to lowercase as it assigned it to the *v_name* variable. The second example uses the concatenate function (represented by two double-bars like ||) to format the output by adding a carriage return between the text fields. We also have PL/SQL functions like the *dbms_output.put_line* procedure that will trim off white space.

```
dbms_output.put_line ('    This has spaces.   ');
```

The leading and training spaces will be removed when placed in the buffer.

Just like in SQL, dates are actually stored in variables as a type of number. This does not mean that a date can be treated as a number, but it does allows you to perform date math and use the date functions in PL\SQL just like a SQL statement. It is common to encounter dates as strings which will require the *to_date* function to convert the string to an actual date variable.

```
d_date1 date := '25-Jan-2005';  -- fails
d_date2 date := to_date('Jan-25-2005','MON-DD-YYYY');
v_date      varchar2(30) := to_char(sysdate);  -- date to string
```

This book does not cover the Oracle-provided built-in functions of SQL, but we will be looking at some PL/SQL functions. If you need help with SQL functions please refer to Chapter 2 of the companion book: *Easy Oracle SQL*.

Variable Declaration Using Database Objects

In the examples so far we have declared variables as a separate object using one of PL/SQL's standard datatypes. Normally a PL/SQL variable is closely tied to a database object and uses the same datatype. For example, if the variable will hold the book title from the *book* table, the variable definition must be of the exact same type and size as the table column. But what happens when the DBA changes the *book* table so that *book_title* is defined as a varchar2(60) instead of a varchar2(40)? It's important to program in such a way that when the tables are changed, the PL/SQL code does not always need to be changed. To get this independence, Oracle has provided a method to declare a variable using the database object the data is based on. To execute this use the *%type* declaration.

```
v_auth_name author.author_last_name%type;
```

The above declaration creates a variable called *v_auth_name* that has the same type definition as the *author_last_name* column in the *author* table. Since the PL/SQL variable is declared when the PL/SQL is executed (a process called "late binding" or "runtime binding"), the variable will always match the type definition of the *author_last_name* column in the database. In plain English, all changes to the type definition in the database are automatically applied to the PL/SQL variable. You can also create records using the *%rowtype* declaration.

```
r_auth  author%rowtype;
```

The variable *r_auth* (r_ is for record) is declared as a record that will hold one row from the author table. If the DBA adds a column to the author table in the database, the record *r_auth* will automatically include the new column. The PL/SQL block continues to function correctly after the change. Of course, if my code needs to use the new column, then the code will need to be

---

updated. The example below selects data from the database and stores it in the variables defined.

```
SQL> declare
  2    r_auth author%rowtype;
  3    v_last_name author.author_last_name%type;
  4  begin
  5    select * into r_auth
  6    from author
  7    where author_key = 'A101';
  8
  9    select author_last_name into v_last_name
 10    from author
 11    where author_key = 'A101';
 12
 13    dbms_output.put_line ('Name: '||
 14                          r_auth. author_last_name);
 15    dbms_output.put_line ('Name: '||v_last_name);
 16  end;
 17  /

Name: jones
Name: jones
```

Notice that if the DBA adds a column to the *author* table, the block still executes without problem because the row is defined using the %rowtype declaration. If the DBA changes the size of the *author_last_name* column, the block picks up the change when the *v_last_name* variable is declared because it used *%type*.

The internal variables in a record are accessed using the "dot" notation. In the example a row was retrieved into the record *r_auth*. To get the author last name from the record, use the "*record.column_name*".

```
dbms_output.put_line ('Name: '||
                      r_auth. author_last_name);
```

Since the record is defined as *author%rowtype*, it contains an entry for every column in the author table. If the column is null in the table, it will be null in the record. Anytime variables interact with the data in the database, they should be defined using *%type* or *%rowtype*.

Assignments, Initializations and NULLs

We have already seen that the assignment operator is the colon equal (:=) syntax and we have seen how this is used to assign values to a variable both within the code and upon declaration. It is a good practice to initialize variables to a value when they are declared. This is especially important with number variables to avoid null math errors.

Many programming languages avoid NULLs by requiring that a variable be initialized before use. However, in a database, NULLs are commonly used and are not considered errors. Anytime a row is inserted into a table with only some of the column values defined, NULLs are used for the undefined columns. Thus NULLs are values in the database.

The value of NULL is 'undefined'. That means it is not zero, or one, or anything. It is undefined. Because the value of NULL is undefined it can be tricky to work with.

Did you say Null Math or Dull Math?

Null math is using any NULL value in a mathematical equation. Null math always returns a NULL. This is a simply concept, but NULL math is a very common PL/SQL bug.

```
SQL> declare
  2    n_1 number;   -- null
  3    n_2 number := 0;
  4    n_3 number := 1;
  5  begin
  6    dbms_output.put_line ('Addition:        '|| n_1 + 5);
  7    dbms_output.put_line ('Subtraction:     '|| n_1 - 5);
  8    dbms_output.put_line ('Multiplication: '|| n_1 * 5);
  9    dbms_output.put_line ('Division:        '|| n_1 + 5);
 10  end;
 11  /
declare
*
ERROR at line 1:
ORA-06502: PL/SQL: numeric or value error: character to
number conversion error
ORA-06512: at line 6
```

The example above fails when *dbms_output.out_line* attempts to convert *n_1 + 5* from a number to a character because it has the value of NULL.

In the example below, the value of *n_2* is shown. Notice that there is no value when *n_1* is added because it is NULL.

```
SQL> declare
  2    n_1 number;   -- null
  3    n_2 number := 0;
  4    n_3 number := 1;
  5  begin
  6    n_2 := n_2 + n_3;
  7    dbms_output.put_line ('Results: '|| n_2);
  8    n_2 := n_1 + n_3;
  9    dbms_output.put_line ('Results: '|| n_2);
 10  end;
 11  /

Results: 1
Results:
```

This is a very common code bug and it can be hard to locate. So with PL/SQL, the developer must contend not only with division by zero, but also null math.

NULLs can also be problematic with comparisons. Since NULL is undefined the developer must insure that the correct comparison is used. In the example below, n_1 is a null while n_2 is a number.

```
n_1 number;              -- null
n_2 number := 4;
```

A comparison results in a true or a false. Here are some comparisons using the variables above.

```
(n_2 > 2)     true;   --4>2.
(n_1 > 2)     false; --null>2 undefined therefore false.
(n_1 < n_2)   false; --null < 4;
                            undefined therefore false.
(n_1 = n_2)   false; --null = 4;
                            undefined therefore false.
(n_1 <> n_2)  true;   --null <> 4;
                       undefined is not equal to 4.
```

No matter how *n_1* is used in the comparison, it is still an undefined comparison and therefore false, except if the "not equal" comparison is used. The "not equal" comparison returns true because undefined can never be equal to a value. This is important in the if/then and loop flow control discussed in chapter two. If the developer selects the wrong comparison, it may return a "false" due to a variable not being initialized or return a "true" using the "not equal" comparison. If the variable *n_x* has not been initialized then the following will always branch to the ELSE clause.

```
if (n_x < 10)
  then v_line := 'Never get here';
else v_line := 'always end up here';
end if;
```

The variable *v_line* will always be 'always end up here' because n_x < 10 will always be false.

```
if (n_x <> 10)
  then v_line := 'this is true';
else v_line := 'this is false';
end if;
```

In the above example, *v_line* will always be 'this is true' because n_x <> 10 will always be true. If this is the behavior desired then the code will work. It will be very confusing to the code maintainer, who has to figure out what the initial coder was trying to accomplish. You should use PL/SQL's natural language structure to make code understandable and avoid "tricks" that accomplish a task but are confusing or difficult to understand. If the code is confusing to read, it's going to be hard to maintain. Good PL/SQL developers get in the habit of using comments to explain what actions are being performed and why you are making calculations. Next we will examine nested blocks and learn about the "scope" of PL/SQL variables.

Nested Blocks and Variable Scope

As stated earlier, a PL/SQL block contains a *declare* section and a code section. A block can contain other blocks and these blocks are termed nested blocks. A nested block may have an optional declare and exception section. A nested block is seen as a single statement to the outer block.

A variable defined in the declare section of a block can be seen by all the statements in the block to include the nested blocks. This is referred to as the variable's scope.

The example below demonstrates when the two variables go in and out of scope.

```
SQL> declare
  2    v_title book.book_title%type;
  3  begin
  4    v_title := 'Easy Oracle SQL';   -- in scope
  5
  6    declare -- a nested block
  7      v_title2 book.book_title%type;
  8    begin
  9      v_title2 := 'Easy Oracle PL/SQL';  -- in scope
 10      v_title := 'Painful Oracle SQL';   -- in scope
```

```
11      end;
12
13      dbms_output.put_line (v_title);   -- in scope
14      dbms_output.put_line (v_title2); -- failed
15  end;
16  /

 dbms_output.put_line (v_title2); -- failed
                              *
ERROR at line 14:
ORA-06550: line 14, column 24:
PLS-00201: identifier 'V_TITLE2' must be declared
ORA-06550: line 14, column 3:
PL/SQL: Statement ignored
```

The second output (line 14) fails because *v_title2* is defined in the nested block and is out of scope in the outer block. The procedure *dbms_output.put_line* can not see the variable because it was defined in the nested block and the output line is in the outer block. Also the nested block is able to change the variable *v_title* because it is still in scope in the nested block. If a variable is declared in a nested block that is also declared in the outer block, the variable in the nested block is a new variable and the variable in the outer block is not in scope in the nested block.

Remember, two variables of the same name cannot be "in scope" at the same time. Defining a new variable with the same name as an existing variable will cause the existing variable to go out of scope as long as the new variable is in scope. This is demonstrated in the example below.

```
SQL> declare
  2      v_title book.book_title%type;
  3  begin
  4      v_title := 'Easy Oracle SQL';   -- in scope
  5
  6      declare -- a nested block
  7        v_title book.book_title%type;
  8      begin
  9        v_title := 'Easy Oracle PL/SQL';  -- in scope
 10        dbms_output.put_line (v_title);   -- in scope
 11      end;
 12
 13      dbms_output.put_line (v_title); -- in scope
 14  end;
 15  /
```

The first declaration for *v_title* in the outer block is assigned the value *'Easy Oracle SQL'* in line 4. The nested block also declares a variable called *v_title* in line 7. This creates a new variable for the nested block and the outer *v_title* variable goes out of scope. The nested block assigns *'Easy Oracle PL/SQL'* to the *v_title* variable in line 9 and outputs it to the buffer.

The nested block ends so the nested *v_title* variable goes out of scope and the outer *v_title* comes back in scope. Hence the second time *v_title* is written to the buffer in line 13, it contains the original assignment.

Conclusion

This Chapter was an introduction to what PL/SQL is and how to use it. After introducing PL/SQL, the installation of the pubs database and basic introduction to SQL*Plus, PL/SQL blocks were discussed and PL/SQL variables were introduced.

PL/SQL is an easy to read, strongly type, portable programming language that executes within an Oracle database. It is Oracle dependent and will not run in any other vendor's database management system. PL/SQL is tightly coupled to the SQL language and is very efficient at manipulating data stored in the database. PL/SQL executes within the database rather than on a client computer or application server.

PL/SQL is based on blocks that have a declarative section and procedural section. The declarative section is used to define variables and other objects used in the block. The procedural section contains the statements that perform the work. It is surrounded by a *begin* and *end* statement. It may also have an *exception* section to handle exceptions that arise inside the block.

Unnamed PL/SQL blocks are called anonymous blocks. They are not stored in the database but are sent to the database for execution. Named blocks are called procedures and functions. A PL/SQL procedure accepts variables and performs a task, while PL/SQL functions accept variables, perform a task and always returns a value.

Variables are declared in the declarative section of a PL/SQL block. Their scope is the block they are declared in, plus any nested block. Variables declared in a nested block can not be seen outside of the nested block. Variables can be any standard Oracle defined type or a user defined type. Any variables that will hold data from, or pass data to the database should be declared using the database object's defined type, using the *%type* and *%rowtype* declaration. This allows the variable to adapt to a change in the database object.

The next chapter builds on what has been discussed and adds program control structure. From variable testing using if/then structures to a whole set of loop command, the next chapter will present controlling how and where a program branches.

At this point you should have an understanding of PL/SQL blocks, in Chapter 2 *Flow Control* we put anonymous PL/SQL blocks to work and start writing more complex code.

PL/QL Flow Control

PL/SQL Flow Control

Flow control allows the sequence of execution to be altered by some condition, usually an IF statement, and all programming languages implement flow control. In this chapter we discuss PL/SQL's implementation of flow control, focusing on the various IF/THEN conditional statements, followed by the various loop implementations.

In a nutshell, flow control allows the programmer to check a condition, and decide which path the program will take through the code. The condition checked is a Boolean (returning either "true" or "false"). Any PL/SQL evaluation, function, or compound statement can be used in the check condition as long as the result is a Boolean true/false result. In PL/SQL the condition evaluation can be enclosed in parentheses for clarity but that is not a requirement. Let's take a closer look.

IF/THEN/ELSE Statements

The IF/THEN statement checks a Boolean value or expression and if true, executes the statements in the THEN clause. If the condition is false, the statements in the THEN clause are skipped and execution jumps to the END IF, and the expression that is checked must return a true or false. It can be a simple Boolean variable or a compound expression joined with AND/OR clauses, and the expression can even be a PL/SQL function that returns a Boolean value.

There is no requirement to surround the expression with parenthesis but most developers use parentheses for clarity. The THEN clause can contain a single or multiple statements, or a nested PL/SQL block. Here is an example of a basic IF/THEN statement with a THEN clause.

```
if v_numb > 5 then
  v_numb  := 5;
  v_other := 10;
end if;
```

In the statements above, the Boolean condition (*v_numb* > 5) must be true before the THEN clause is executed. If *v_numb* is equal to or less than 5, or if it evaluates to NULL, the program control jumps to the statement after the END IF clause. Note that the THEN clause can contain any number of valid PL/SQL statements. The variable *v_other* and *v_numb* will not change unless the condition is true.

Note: All the IF/THEN statements must end with an END IF clause. The PL/SQL engine will continue to include statements in the THEN clause until it encounters an END IF. If you get a compile error that states: "found xxxx when expecting IF", the compiler encountered an END statement before it encountered the END IF. Simply find the end of you IF statement and close it with an END IF to correct the problem.

Sometimes the program flow will want to branch one direction if the condition is true and another direction if the condition is false, and this is handled within the IF/THEN/ELSE statement.

Like the IF/THEN statement, the THEN clause statements will only be executed if the condition is true. However if the condition is false, the statements in the ELSE clause are executed. This is an either-or situation.

```
if n_numb > 5 then
  v_status := 'large';
else
  v _status := 'small';
end if;
```

After executing the example, the variable *v_status* will be defined as either large or small. Note that the above statement could also be written as two separate IF statements.

```
if n_numb > 5 then v_status := 'large'; end if;
if n_numb <=5 then v_status := 'small'; end if;
```

Programmatically, the results are the same, however the two IF statements required two evaluations, while the IF/THEN/ELSE statement requires only one evaluation. But what if there are multiple IF statements checking for multiple conditions? Let's see an example.

IF/THEN/ELSIF/ELSE

In the example below, a number of IF statements are used.

```
if n_numb = 1 then
   v_status := 'very small';
end if;

if n_numb <= 4  then
   v_status := 'small';
end if;

if n_numb = 5 then
   v_status := 'even';
end if;

if n_numb > 5 then
   v_status := 'large';
end if;

if n_numb = 10 then
   v_status := 'very large';
end if;
```

The set of statements has a number of problems, not the least of which is that some values will satisfy multiple statements. You could fix that problem by reordering the statements. However, all five statements will still have to be evaluated for each run.

By using the ELSIF statement, the program will jump past the remaining evaluations once a true condition is reached.

```
if n_numb = 1 then
   v_status := 'very small';
   elsif
      n_numb < 4 then v_status := 'small';
      elsif
         n_numb = 5 then v_status := 'even';
         elsif
            n_numb < 4 then v_status := 'large';
         else
            v_status := 'very large';
end if;
```

Notice that once the condition evaluates to true, the THEN clause is executed and the control will jump over all other statements to the END IF clause. This method is called a *'short circuit'* evaluation. Also note these features of the syntax:

- The ELSE clause at the end is optional. If we include the final ELSE, the ELSE clause is executed when the conditions above it all evaluate to false.

- Each ELSIF clause must have a condition evaluation and a THEN clause.

- The ELSE clause has no condition evaluation and the THEN key word is omitted.

The THEN clause can contain any series of valid PL/SQL statements including calling procedures, functions, nested blocks of code, or nested IF statements.

```
SQL> declare
  2    n_temp number(8,2) := &Temp_f;
  3    v_results varchar2(40);
  4  begin
  5    -- Change from Fahrenheit to Celsius
  6    n_temp := (5/9)*(n_temp -32);
  7
```

```
 8    if n_temp > 40
 9      then v_results := 'WARM';
10    elsif n_temp <= 40 and n_temp > 0
11      then v_results := 'Cold';
12    else v_results := 'Very Cold';
13    end if;
14
15    dbms_output.put_line ('The Temp Outside is '||v_results);
16    dbms_output.put_line ('It is '||n_temp||' C.');
17  end;
18  /
Enter value for temp_f: 55
The Temp Outside is Cold
It is 12.78 C.

PL/SQL procedure successfully completed.

SQL> /

Enter value for temp_f: 5
The Temp Outside is Very Cold
It is -15 C.
```

In the example above, a SQL*Plus variable is passed to the anonymous block (verify was turned off with the SQL*Plus command 'set verify off'). The temperature contained in the variable *Temp_f* is in Fahrenheit. It is converted on line 6 to degrees Celsius. Lines 8 through 13 use the IF statement to define how cold it is. The results are then printed out using the *dbms_output.put_line* procedure. Notice that the ELSIF clause on line 10 uses a compound condition with the AND keyword. The compound condition can contain as many evaluations as needed as long as the entire evaluate ends up either true or false. Now, let's look at some more complex Boolean operations with multiple logical operators.

Multiple Logical Operators

The PL/SQL language is very powerful and any IF condition evaluation can consist of multiple comparisons, joined together by logical operators. In the next example, the IF condition on line 6 contains three evaluations, joined by the AND/OR logical operators.

```
SQL> declare
  2    n_test number := &Entry;
  3    n_10   number := 10;
  4    n_100  number := 100;
  5  begin
  6    if (n_test < n_100 and n_test > n_10 or n_test = 5)
  7      then dbms_output.put_line ('True');
  8    else dbms_output.put_line ('False');
  9    end if;
 10  end;
 11  /
Enter value for entry: 25
old    2:    n_test number := &Entry;
new    2:    n_test number := 25;
True

PL/SQL procedure successfully completed.

SQL> /
Enter value for entry: 5
old    2:    n_test number := &Entry;
new    2:    n_test number := 5;
True

PL/SQL procedure successfully completed.

SQL> /
Enter value for entry: 6
old    2:    n_test number := &Entry;
new    2:    n_test number := 6;
False
```

When using multiple conditions, the conditions are evaluated in the same order as in an SQL statement's WHERE clause, with all ANDs, then all ORs are evaluated from left-to-right. To demonstrate this I made a change in the example below so that the AND evaluation results in a false condition. Please hand-execute this code:

```
SQL> declare
  2    n_test number := &Entry;
  3    n_10   number := 10;
  4    n_100  number := 100;
  5  begin
  6    if (n_test > n_100 and n_test > n_10 or n_test = 5)
  7      then dbms_output.put_line ('True');
  8    else dbms_output.put_line ('False');
  9    end if;
 10  end;
 11  /
```

```
Enter value for entry: 5
old   2:   n_test number := &Entry;
new   2:   n_test number := 5;
True
```

In this example we see that the ANDs evaluated to "false", but the OR was tested last and the overall statement evaluated to "true".

When evaluating large numbers of conditions, the IF/THEN/ELSIF/ELSE statements can become long and confusing. Using a CASE statement may make your code more understandable and less error prone.

If I figure this out, then my program will run, else my program will not run and I lose my job.

The PL/SQL CASE Statement

The CASE statement was introduced in Oracle8i SQL, but it was not until Oracle9i that we could use the CASE statement inside PL/SQL. The CASE statement is like a series of IF statements, only using the key word WHEN. A CASE statement is evaluated from top to bottom. If a condition is true, then corresponding

THEN clause is executed and execution jumps to the END CASE (short circuit evaluation) clause.

```
case
when n_numb = 1 then v_status := 'very small';
when n_numb < 4 then v_status := 'small';
when n_numb = 5 then v_status := 'even';
when n_numb > 4 then v_status := 'large';
else v_status := 'very large';
end case;
```

Note that the ELSE clause is optional, but it is similar to the IF statement because the CASE statement must end with an END CASE clause.

```
SQL> declare
  2    n_numb    number := &Entry;
  3    v_status varchar2(40);
  4  begin
  5
  6    case
  7      when n_numb = 1
  8        then v_status := 'very small';
  9      when n_numb < 4
 10        then v_status := 'small';
 11      when n_numb = 5
 12        then v_status := 'even';
 13      when n_numb < 4
 14        then v_status := 'large';
 15    else v_status := 'very large';
 16    end case;
 17
 18    dbms_output.put_line ('Status: '|| v_status);
 19  end;
 20  /

Enter value for entry: 3
old   2:   n_numb    number := &Entry;
new   2:   n_numb    number := 3;
Status: small

SQL> /
Enter value for entry: 1
old   2:   n_numb    number := &Entry;
new   2:   n_numb    number := 1;
Status: very small
```

Notice that on the second run, the entered value was 1. The condition on line 7 was true, the status was set and execution jumped to line 12. Had the statement in line 8 executed, its condition would also evaluate to true and the status would have been set to 'small'. Thus, once a condition evaluates to true, the corresponding THEN clause is executed, and the code execution jumps to the END CASE clause.

Each WHEN clause in the CASE statement executes a separate evaluation and the evaluation need not use the same formula or variables.

```
SQL> declare
  2    n_1 number := &Entry;
  3    n_2 number := 0;
  4    n_3 number := 4;
  5    v_results varchar2(40);
  6  begin
  7    case
  8      when (n_1 + n_2 > 10)
  9        then v_results := 'Case 1 true';
 10      when ((n_1 + 6) < 10)
 11        then v_results := 'Case 2 true';
 12      when ((n_2*n_3) < 5)
 13        then v_results := 'Case 3 true';
 14      else v_results := 'No case is true';
 15    end case;
 16
 17    dbms_output.put_line (v_results);
 18  end;
 19  /
Enter value for entry: 3
old   2:    n_1 number := &Entry;
new   2:    n_1 number := 3;
Case 2 true

SQL> /
Enter value for entry: 11
old   2:    n_1 number := &Entry;
new   2:    n_1 number := 11;
Case 1 true

SQL> /
Enter value for entry: 5
old   2:    n_1 number := &Entry;
new   2:    n_1 number := 5;
Case 3 true
```

In the above example each WHEN clause has a condition that test a different set of variables. Again, the case exhibits the short circuit evaluation, with execution jumping to the END CASE clause once a condition evaluates as true and the corresponding THEN clause is executed.

If all the conditions evaluate to false and there is no ELSE clause a CASE_NOT_FOUND exception is raised. Exceptions are covered in Chapter 3, "Procedures, Functions and Exception Handling". Another form of the CASE statement evaluates a single expression against a set of results.

```
SQL> declare
  2    n_numb    number := &Entry;
  3    v_results varchar2(40);
  4  begin
  5    case n_numb
  6      when 3 then v_results := 'very small';
  7      when 4 then v_results := 'small';
  8      when 5 then v_results := 'even';
  9      when 6 then v_results := 'large';
 10    else v_results := 'Not a valid value';
 11    end case;
 12
 13    dbms_output.put_line (v_results);
 14  end;
 15  /
Enter value for entry: 3
old   2:   n_numb    number := &Entry;
new   2:   n_numb    number := 3;
very small


SQL> /
Enter value for entry: 6
old   2:   n_numb    number := &Entry;
new   2:   n_numb    number := 6;
large

SQL> /
Enter value for entry: 8
old   2:   n_numb    number := &Entry;
new   2:   n_numb    number := 8;
Not a valid value
```

Here the variable *n_numb* is evaluated against the numbers in the WHEN clause. Using the CASE statement is neither more nor less efficient than the IF/THEN/ELSIF/ELSE. It should be used to improve the readability or maintainability of your code.

The PL/SQL GOTO Statement

The GOTO statement is an unconditional branch that will jump execution to the "label" identified in the statement. It is not used very often and some programmers claim you should never use the GOTO statement as it will make the code harder to understand and violates the structured programming paradigm. A label is defined in the code with double open and close brackets.

```
<< important_label >>
```

When a GOTO statement is encountered, program execution jumps to the code directly after the label, so there must be at least one line of code after the label. Likewise, the label must be in scope when the GOTO statement is encountered. This requirement makes the GOTO statement a lot less useful than it appears. For example the first GOTO statements below are in scope with the labels.

```
SQL> declare
  2    n_numb number := &Number;
  3  begin
  4    if n_numb < 5 then goto small_number;
  5    else goto large_number;
  6    end if;
  7
  8    n_numb := 25; -- goto jumps this line.
  9
 10    <<small_number>>
 11    dbms_output.put_line('Small Number.');
 12    goto end_message;
 13
 14    <<large_number>>
 15    dbms_output.put_line('Large Number.');
 16    goto end_message;
 17
 18    n_numb := 0;  -- goto jumps this line.
 19
 20    <<end_message>>
 21    dbms_output.put_line('The End.');
 22
 23  end;
 24  /
```

```
Enter value for number: 4
Small Number.
The End.

SQL> /
Enter value for number: 7
Large Number.
The End.
```

However, the example below shows that objects declared within the IF statements are out of scope to the outside block of code.

```
SQL> declare
  2    n_num number := 5;
  3  begin
  4    goto then_clause;
  5    if  n_num < 8
  6      then
  7        <<then_clause>>
  8        n_num := 8;
  9    end if;
 10  end;
 11  /

 goto then_clause;
   *
ERROR at line 4:
ORA-06550: line 4, column 3:
PLS-00375: illegal GOTO statement;
this GOTO cannot branch to label
'THEN_CLAUSE'
ORA-06550: line 6, column 5:
PL/SQL: Statement ignored
```

Jumping out of the IF statement in the first example is allowed because the label is in scope. Jumping into an IF statement in the second example is not allowed because the label is not in scope. This is also true for LOOPs, CASE statements, and PL/SQL exceptions. Likewise, a label in a function or procedure is not in scope to the calling block.

The PL/SQL NULL Statement

Sometimes PL/SQL requires a code statement when you may not have anything to execute. Use of a nonsense statement is

---

possible, but why have the server calculate or compare a value for no reason. This is when you use the NULL statement.

Remember that one of the requirements of the GOTO statement is that there is a least one line of code after the label.

```
SQL> declare
  2     n_num number := 5;
  3  begin
  4     goto then_clause;
  5     n_num := 3;
  6     <<then_clause>>
  7  end;
  8  /
end;
*
ERROR at line 7:
ORA-06550: line 7, column 1:
PLS-00103: Encountered the symbol "END" when expecting one of the
following:
```

What if you want to end the code block? You could add a "nonsense" code line. A nonsense code line is a piece of code that never performs any action.

Line 7 in the example below is a nonsense code example.

```
SQL> declare
  2     n_num number := 5;
  3  begin
  4     goto then_clause;
  5     n_num := 3;
  6     <<then_clause>>
  7     if 4=7 then n_num := 5; end if;
  8  end;
  9  /

PL/SQL procedure successfully completed.
```

As we see, line 7 will never execute (4 will never equal 7) but the server will have to compare 4=7 every time it hits that statement. It is better to just use the NULL statement.

```
SQL> declare
  2    n_num number := 5;
  3  begin
  4    goto then_clause;
  5    n_num := 3;
  6    <<then_clause>>
  7    null;
  8  end;
  9  /

PL/SQL procedure successfully completed.
```

The NULL statement can also be used to iteratively create a large section of code. Many developers like to build complicated code segments by building the skeleton (or stems) and then expanding each section one piece at a time, compiling and testing at each step.

```
SQL> declare
  2    n_numb number := 4;
  3  begin
  4    -- check for valid value
  5    begin
  6      if n_numb < 0 AND n_numb > 10
  7        then goto invalid_number;
  8      end if;
  9    end;
 10    --  compute the requirements
 11    begin
 12    end;
 13    -- handle invalid numbers
 14    <<invalid_number>>
 15    begin
 16    end;
 17  end;
 18  /
  end;
  *
ERROR at line 12:
ORA-06550: line 12, column 3:
PLS-00103: Encountered the symbol "END" when expecting one of the
following: …
```

The PL/SQL engine does not like the BEGIN and END statements on lines 11 and 12. It will have the same problem with lines 15 and 16. Use the NULL statement to allow this partially completed code to compile and execute.

```
SQL> declare
  2    n_numb number := 4;
  3  begin
  4    -- check for valid value
  5    begin
  6      if n_numb < 0 AND n_numb > 10
  7        then goto invalid_number;
  8      end if;
  9    end;
 10    --  compute the requirements
 11    begin
 12      null;
 13    end;
 14    -- handle invalid numbers
 15    <<invalid_number>>
 16    begin
 17      null;
 18    end;
 19  end;
 20  /
```

Like the IF/THEN statement, the LOOP is another common flow control structure that all programming languages implement. PL/SQL implements three loop structures; the endless loop, the WHILE loop and the FOR loop. The loop boundaries are defined by the key words LOOP and END LOOP. These never-ending WHILE loops are referred to as "indeterminate loops" because they continue to loop forever until a condition causes the loop to exit. This is in contrast to a FOR loop, a "determinate loop" that executes for a specified number of iterations.

Uses for Endless Looping

An endless loop has no bounds in its definition. It will loop forever until a statement causes program control to jump out of the loop. The EXIT WHEN (condition = true) statement is normally used to terminate an endless loop. When the condition evaluates to true, program control jumps out of the loop, continuing from the END LOOP statement.

If the EXIT WHEN (condition = true) statement never evaluates to true, the program will continue to loop forever. This will make the database administrator very unhappy.

He could have just told me I had an endless loop problem!

```
SQL> declare
  2    n_numb number := 1;
  3  begin
  4    loop
  5      dbms_output.put_line ('Number is '||n_numb);
  6      n_numb := n_numb + 1;
  7      exit when n_numb < 1;   -- never happen
  8    end loop;
  9  end;
 10  /
Number is 1
Number is 2
Number is 3
Number is 4
Number is 5
Number is 6
Number is 7
...
Number is 121
Number is 122
Number is 123
Number is 124
declare
*
ERROR at line 1:
ORA-20000: ORU-10027: buffer overflow, limit of 2000 bytes
ORA-06512: at "SYS.DBMS_OUTPUT", line 35
ORA-06512: at "SYS.DBMS_OUTPUT", line 198
ORA-06512: at "SYS.DBMS_OUTPUT", line 139
ORA-06512: at line 5
```

In the above example, the EXIT WHEN (condition = true) will never evaluate to true and the loop will continue forever. What stopped the loop in the example above is that *dbms_output.put_line* procedure places the output in a buffer, that SQL*Plus retrieves after the block completes. The output filled the buffer and caused a buffer overflow exception, which terminated processing. If the buffer had not terminated the loop, the database administrator would have to kill the process from in the database. Fixing the EXIT WHEN (condition = true) results in the desired output.

```
SQL> declare
  2     n_numb number := 1;
  3   begin
  4     loop
  5        dbms_output.put_line ('Number is '||n_numb);
  6        n_numb := n_numb + 1;
  7        exit when n_numb > 10;   -- fixed
  8     end loop;
  9   end;
 10   /
Number is 1
Number is 2
Number is 3
Number is 4
Number is 5
Number is 6
Number is 7
Number is 8
Number is 9
Number is 10

PL/SQL procedure successfully completed.
```

The EXIT WHEN (condition = true) statement exits immediately. If you need to set values before exiting, use the plain EXIT statement. The EXIT statement will exit without checking a condition. The EXIT statement is normally found after some other flow control statement which checks the exit condition.

```
SQL> declare
  2    n_numb number := 1;
  3  begin
  4    loop
  5      dbms_output.put_line ('Number is '||n_numb);
  6      n_numb := n_numb + 1;
  7      if n_numb > 10
  8        then
  9          dbms_output.put_line ('Exiting the loop.');
 10          exit;
 11      end if;
 12    end loop;
 13  end;
 14  /
Number is 1
Number is 2
Number is 3
Number is 4
Number is 5
Number is 6
Number is 7
Number is 8
Number is 9
Number is 10
Exiting the loop.
```

Where the EXIT WHEN (condition = true) statement is placed in the loop code is important to insure that you exit the loop in the appropriate place, such as exiting before or after a variable is changed. Placing the EXIT WHEN (condition = true) statement at the start of the loop simulates a WHILE loop, placing it at the end of the loop simulates a "loop until" construct (the "loop until" is not implemented in PL/SQL). The endless loop starts executing and then tests the condition for exit. The WHILE loop test the condition first, then executes the loop only while the condition remains true.

The PL/SQL WHILE Loop

The WHILE loop, also called a conditional loop, evaluates a condition before each loop executes, and if false, the loop is terminated. If the expression is false when the program reaches the WHILE loop, the loop code is jumped and never executed. Use a WHILE loop when the condition test is required at the start of the loop. The next example contains three WHILE loops.

```
SQL> declare
  2    v_test varchar2(8) := 'RUN';
  3    n_numb number := 2;
  4  begin
  5    while v_test <> 'STOP' loop
  6      if n_numb > 5
  7        then v_test := 'STOP';
  8        end if;
  9      dbms_output.put_line (v_test||': '||n_numb);
 10      n_numb := n_numb + 1;
 11    end loop;
 12
 13    v_test := 'DOWN';
 14    while n_numb > 1 AND v_test = 'DOWN' loop
 15      dbms_output.put_line (v_test||': '||n_numb);
 16      n_numb := n_numb - 1;
 17    end loop;
 18
 19    while 7 = 4 loop
 20      NULL;  -- never get here
 21    end loop;
 22  end;
 23  /
RUN:  2
RUN:  3
RUN:  4
RUN:  5
STOP:  6
DOWN:  7
DOWN:  6
DOWN:  5
DOWN:  4
DOWN:  3
DOWN:  2
```

The last loop will never execute because the condition will never be true. The middle loop uses multiple condition tests, using the AND key word. The first loop runs while *v_test* does not equal 'STOP'. Notice that the check that changes *v_test* in lines 6, 7, 8 is at the top of the loop. This is a poor choice because even though *v_test* may change, it is not evaluated again until the program gets back to the top of the loop. This results in the output stopping after *n_numb* reached 6, but notice in the results that at completion of the first loop, *n_numb* was left with a value of 7. Unless this was the programmer's intent, a small, hard to locate bug has been introduced into the code.

The programmer must ensure that the order of the statements inside the loop will leave the variables in the required state when the loop terminates. Remember that the WHILE loop tests at the start of the loop and does not test again until the loop has completely run and returned to the loop start. Both the endless loop and the WHILE loop execute until a condition is met. These loops are effective if the programmer does not know how many times the loop will execute. If the loop will run for a specified number of iterations, it is more efficient to use a FOR loop.

The PL/SQL REPEAT-UNTIL Loop

The WHILE loop test at the start of the loop and it the condition is false, the loop code is never executed. If you want to ensure that the loop code is executed at least one, the test must be preformed at the bottom of the loop. This is referred to as a REPEAT-UNTIL or DO-WHILE loop. PL/SQL does not directly implement a REPEAT-UNTIL loop however it is easy to construct one using an endless loop. By placing the EXIT WHEN (condition = true) statement as the last line of code in an endless loop you will achieve the same results.

```
SQL> declare
  2    n_num number := 1;
  3  begin
  4    loop
  5      dbms_output.put(n_num||', ');
  6      n_num := n_num + 1;
  7      exit when n_num > 5;
  8    end loop;
  9    dbms_output.put_line('Final: '||n_num);
 10  end;
 11  /
1, 2, 3, 4, 5, Final: 6

PL/SQL procedure successfully completed.
```

Since the condition test is at the bottom of the loop, you ensure that the loop code is executed at least once.

The PL/SQL FOR Loop

The FOR loop executes for a specified number of times, defined in the loop definition. Because the number of loops is specified, the overhead of checking a condition to exit is eliminated. The number of executions is defined in the loop definition as a range from a start value to an end value (inclusive). The integer index in the FOR loop starts at the start value and increments by one (1) for each loop until it reaches the end value.

```
SQL> begin
  2     for idx in 2..5 loop
  3        dbms_output.put_line (idx);
  4     end loop;
  5  end;
  6  /
  2
  3
  4
  5

PL/SQL procedure successfully completed.
```

In the example below a variable *idx* is defined, assigning it the value 100. When the FOR loop executes, the variable *idx* is also defined as the index for the FOR loop. The original variable *idx* goes out of scope when the FOR loop defines its index variable. Inside the FOR loop, the *idx* variable is the loop index. Once the FOR loop terminates, the loop index goes out of scope and the original *idx* variable is again in scope.

```
SQL> declare
  2     idx number := 100;
  3  begin
  4     dbms_output.put_line (idx);
  5     for idx in 2..5 loop
  6        dbms_output.put_line (idx);
  7     end loop;
  8     dbms_output.put_line (idx);
```

```
  9  end;
 10  /
100
2
3
4
5
100

PL/SQL procedure successfully completed.
```

You can use the loop index inside the loop, but you can not change it. If you want to loop by an increment other than one, you will have to do so programmatically as the FOR loop will only increment the index by one.

```
SQL> begin
  2     for i in 4 .. 200 loop
  3        i := i + 4;
  4     end loop;
  5  end;
  6  /
     i := i + 4;
     *
ERROR at line 3:
ORA-06550: line 3, column 5:
PLS-00363: expression 'I' cannot be used as an assignment target
ORA-06550: line 3, column 5:
PL/SQL: Statement ignored
```

The loop index start and stop values can be expressions or variables. They are evaluated once at the start of the loop to determine the number of loop iterations. If their values change during the loop processing, it does not impact the number of iterations.

```
SQL> declare
  2     n_start number := 3;
  3     n_stop  number := 6;
  4  begin
  5     for xyz in n_start .. n_stop loop
  6        n_stop := 100;
  7        dbms_output.put_line (xyz);
  8     end loop;
  9  end;
 10  /
```

```
  3
  4
  5
  6

PL/SQL procedure successfully completed.
```

Line 6 changes the stop value, setting it to 100. But the loop still terminates at the value of 6. The loop index start and stop values are always defined from lowest to highest. If you want the index to count down use the REVERSE key word.

```
SQL> begin
  2    for num in 4 .. 7 loop
  3      dbms_output.put_line (num);
  4    end loop;
  5
  6    for num in reverse 4 .. 7 loop
  7      dbms_output.put_line (num);
  8    end loop;
  9
 10    for num in 7 .. 4 loop
 11      dbms_output.put_line (num);
 12    end loop;
 13  end;
 14  /
  4
  5
  6
  7
  7
  6
  5
  4

PL/SQL procedure successfully completed.
```

Notice that the third FOR loop COMPILED BUT DID NOT EXECUTE! The FOR loop calculated the number of loop iterations and got a negative number, therefore the loop count was zero.

In the next example a FOR loop is used to calculate the factorial of a number. A factorial value is commonly used to determine all possible values for a number and is defined as $x*(x-1)*(x-2)....(0) = !x$.

```
!8 = 8*7*6*5*4*3*2*1 = 40320

SQL> declare
  2     v_seed number := &numb;
  3     v_hold number := 1;
  4  begin
  5     for i in reverse 1 .. v_seed loop
  6        v_hold := v_hold * i;
  7     end loop;
  8     dbms_output.put_line ('!'||v_seed||' = '||v_hold);
  9  end;
 10  /

Enter value for numb: 8
!8 = 40320

SQL> /
Enter value for numb: 4
!4 = 24
```

Notice that the variable *v_hold* is given an initial value of 1. This is important because if it were not initialized it would start with a NULL value and the code would return NULL due to NULL math (refer to the Null Math section in Chapter 1, "Introduction to PL/SQL"). Likewise if a value is initialized to 0, the code would be multiplying by zero (0) always resulting in zero (0).

```
SQL> declare
  2     v_seed number := &numb;
  3     v_hold number;
  4  begin
  5     for i in reverse 1 .. v_seed loop
  6        v_hold := v_hold * i;
  7     end loop;
  8     dbms_output.put_line ('!'||v_seed||' = '||v_hold);
  9  end;
 10  /
Enter value for numb: 4
!4 =        -- (NULL)

SQL> declare
  2     v_seed number := &numb;
  3     v_hold number := 0;
  4  begin
  5     for i in reverse 1 .. v_seed loop
  6        v_hold := v_hold * i;
  7     end loop;
  8     dbms_output.put_line ('!'||v_seed||' = '||v_hold);
  9  end;
 10  /
```

```
Enter value for numb:  4
!4 = 0    -- (multiplication by 0)
```

Improper Loop Termination

Just because you can do something, doesn't mean you should do it. When a loop is implemented in PL/SQL it should terminate in the designed manner. The PL/SQL WHILE loops terminate when the test condition becomes false, and FOR loops terminate after the defined number of iterations. The EXIT and EXIT WHEN (condition = true) statements will exit all loops but should only be used on endless loops. If you find that you need them on a FOR or WHILE loop, you have probably chosen the wrong loop structure to implement.

The GOTO statement should never be used inside a loop to jump out of the loop. Using the GOTO statement to terminate a loop will make your code harder to understand and more difficult to maintain.

Conclusion

This chapter dealt with structures that alter the program flow. All the structures discussed are implemented in almost all programming languages and other than syntax, operate basically the same.

The chapter started by introducing the set of IF statements. We saw that the IF statement implements conditional execution in that if the condition is true the code in the THEN clause is executed. Any of the IF statements that contain an ELSE clause are an either/or condition. Either one of the conditions is true or the code in the ELSE clause is executed.

The GOTO statement is used to jump program execution to the line of code following a label. The label must be in scope when the GOTO statement executes.

The NULL statement does nothing. Its main use is to be a code statement where PL/SQL requires one but the code does not have one.

Loops allow iterative processing of sets of data. PL/SQL implements three types of loops; the endless loop, the WHILE loop and the FOR loop. The endless loop executes until it encounters an EXIT statement or an EXIT WHEN (condition = true) statement is true. A WHILE loop will test a condition and executes the loop until the condition is false, testing again at the start of each loop iteration. The FOR loop executes the loop a defined number of times as specified in the loop definition.

In the next chapter, the skills already covered are put to use in stored procedures and functions. Stored procedures and functions are named blocks of code that can be called by other code. They are compiled and stored in the database. The next chapter will also introduce important error handling capabilities using the exceptions section of the PL/SQL block.

Procedures, Functions and Exception Handling

Procedures, Functions and Exception Handling

In Chapters 1 and 2 the PL/SQL code examples have all been using anonymous or un-named blocks. This chapter introduces two of PL/SQL's named block types, the stored procedure and the function. A third PL/SQL block type, the trigger, is discussed in Chapter 5, *Bulk Operations, Packages and Triggers*. The primary difference between named and unnamed blocks is how the database handles them. When an unnamed block is sent to the database, it compiles and executes that block. When a named block is sent to the database, it compiles and stores the block as a database object. To execute the named block, it must be called.

Procedures and functions allow you to modularize and reuse code. By taking commonly used code and placing it in a separate block, it can be called many times while residing in one location. This allows the developer to create the code once and provides one location where the code is maintained. It also allows the programmer to encapsulate the complexity of the application in easy to understand modules.

Passing Variables

If a procedure or function is going to integrate into an application, it must perform some action that is useful. This means that the application must be able to pass the module information and receive information back. This is accomplished by passing variables to the module that it can use in performing the task. In the case of a procedure, variables can be read, used and changed. A function can read and use a variable, but can not change it (a function returns a value, more on this in a moment). How a procedure uses a variable will be covered shortly, here we just want to discuss how they are passed to the procedure or function.

Variables passed to procedures and functions are defined in the block definition.

```
create procedure full_user_name
  (first_name in  varchar2,
   last_name  in  varchar2,
   full_name  out varchar2)
as
```

This example is the heading of a procedure called *full_user_name* that passes three variables: *first_name*; *last_name*; and *full_name*. These three variable names are used inside the procedure and are in scope only inside the procedure. In the example the variable values are assigned when passed.

```
declare
  v_fullName varchar2(80);
  v_first varchar2(20) := 'Bill';
  v_last  varchar2(40) := 'Smithadoodle';
begin
  full_user_name ('Sam','Smith', v_fullName);
  full_user_name (v_first,v_last,v_fullName);
```

In the code fragment above, the procedure *full_name* is called twice. The first call passes literal values to the procedure, while the second invocation passed predefined variables. The order that the variables are passed is important as PL/SQL will assign them to the procedure's variables in the order that they were passed to the procedure. If the variables are passed out of order, they must be passed by name as in the code fragment below.

```
declare
  v_fullName vatchar2(80);
  v_first varchar2(20) := 'Bill';
  v_last  varchar2(40) := 'Smithadoodle';
begin
  full_user_name (v_last => last_name,
                  v_fullName => full_name,
                  v_first => first_name);
```

Here the parameters are passed out of order and must name the procedure variables they are to be assigned. Passing by name requires that the developer know the name or the variables in the block definition. You can use the DESCRIBE command in SQL*Plus to see the variables and their names. Normally you will pass the variables in order but there are cases when you may want to pass by name. The most common reason to pass a variable by name is to use default values.

Unconstrained Variables

Variables passed to procedures and functions are unconstrained. This allows greater reuse by not limiting the size of the passed variable.

```
create procedure full_name
  (publisher  in  varchar2,
   pub_cost  in  number,
   pub_date  in  date)
```

The *publisher* variable is defined as a varchar2 rather than a size-constrained varchar2(40). This ensures that any varchar2 variable length can be passed to the *publisher* variable.

Default Values

When a variable is defined in a procedure or function, a default value can optionally be assigned. When the procedure is called, the passed variables are assigned in order; those that are not assigned use the default value. If the default values of leading variables should be used, then the variables must be passed by name so that they are correctly assigned to the procedure's variables.

```
SQL> create or replace procedure example_defaults
  2    (n_1 in number := 5,
  3     n_2 in number := 6,
  4     n_3 in number := 7)
  5  as
  6  begin
  7    dbms_output.put_line(n_1||n_2||n_3);
  8  end;
  9  /

Procedure created.
```

The code fragment above defines a procedure called *example_defaults* that has three variables. In the code on line 7, we see that three variables are sent to the buffer for display. The method the programmer uses (e.g. named variable, list of variables) to call the procedure will determine which values are passed and which will use the default values.

```
SQL> begin
  2    example_defaults(7,8,9);
  3    example_defaults(7,8);
  4    example_defaults(7);
  5    example_defaults();
  6  end;
  7  /

789
787
767
567

PL/SQL procedure successfully completed.
```

Notice that the variables are assigned in the order that they appear, and those variables that are not assigned will use their default values. If they are not passed in order, they must be passed by name.

```
SQL> begin
  2    example_defaults(7,8,9);
  3    example_defaults(n_2=>7,n_3=>8);
  4    example_defaults(n_3=>3);
```

Procedures, Functions and Exception Handling

```
  5    example_defaults(n_3=>5);
  6  end;
  7  /

789
578
563
565
```

All the values not passed by name to the procedure will take their default value. If a variable is not assigned a default value, then the call to that procedure must assign it a value or the call will fail.

IN, OUT and INOUT Modes

Values are passed to a procedure in three modes; IN, OUT and INOUT. The mode which a variable is passed defines how the variables can be used inside the procedure. Let's take a closer look at each mode.

IN Mode

A variable passed as mode IN is always read-only. A variable using IN mode can be read and used by the procedure/function but can not be changed and it cannot be the receiver of an assignment operation. Internal to the scope of the procedure or function, variables pass using IN mode can be considered a constant. The IN mode is the default mode to pass a variable, however it is recommended for maintainability reasons to always define the variable passing mode when you define the variable. Variables passed IN can also be assigned a default value as discussed above.

In the example below, three variables are defined as IN variables. Note that on line 7 the code attempts to assign the variable *n_1* the sum of the other two variables. This procedure fails on compile because *n_1* was assigned a mode of IN and therefore can not be used in an assignment.

```
SQL> create or replace procedure example_defaults
  2    (n_1 in number := 5,
  3     n_2 in number := 6,
  4     n_3 in number := 7)
  5  as
  6  begin
  7    n_1 := n_2 + n_3;
  8  end;
  9  /

Warning: Procedure created with compilation errors.

SQL> show errors
Errors for PROCEDURE EXAMPLE_DEFAULTS:

LINE/COL ERROR
-------- ------------------------------------------------
7/3      PLS-00363: expression 'N_1' cannot be used as an assignment
target

7/3      PL/SQL: Statement ignored
```

OUT Mode

A variable passed in OUT mode is used to pass information back from the procedure to the calling program. It is a write-only variable and has no value until the block assigns it a value. Internally, an OUT variable is created and not initialized when the procedure is called. When the procedure ends, the variable value (upon ending) is copied to the variable passed in the call. As such, a variable passed in OUT mode can not be assigned a default value nor can it be read inside the procedure. Because the variable value is copied back to the passed variable when the procedure terminates, the calling code can not pass an OUT variable a literal value. If the procedure raises an exception that is not caught, it will result in the OUT variable not being copied when the procedure terminates.

```
SQL> create or replace procedure example_defaults
  2    (n_1 in number := 5,
  3     n_2 in number := 6,
  4     n_3 out number := 7)
  5  as
  6  begin
  7    null;
```

```
  8  end;
  9  /

Warning: Procedure created with compilation errors.

SQL> show errors
Errors for PROCEDURE EXAMPLE_DEFAULTS:

LINE/COL ERROR
-------- ---------------------------------------------
4/4      PLS-00230: OUT and IN OUT formal parameters may not have
default expressions
```

INOUT Mode

A variable passed in INOUT mode has characteristics of both the IN and the OUT mode. The variable value is passed in and can be read by the procedure. The procedure can also change the value and it will be copied back to the passed variable when the procedure completes. Like a variable passed in OUT mode, an INOUT variable can not have a default value and can not be passed as a literal. If the procedure terminates abnormally (as in an exception) the INOUT variable will not be copied back to the variable passed in.

NOCOPY Clause

The final point to cover in passing variables is the NOCOPY clause. When a parameter is passed as an IN variable, it is passed by reference. Since it will not change, PL/SQL uses the passed variable in the procedure/function. When variables are passed in OUT or INOUT mode, a new variable is define, and the value is copied to the passed variable when the procedure ends. If the variable is a large structure such as a PL/SQL table or an array, the application could see a performance degradation cause by copying this structure.

The NOCOPY clause tells to PL/SQL engine to pass the variable by reference, thus avoiding the cost of copying the variable at the end of the procedure. The PL/SQL engine has requirements that must be met before passing the variable by reference and if those requirements are not met, the NOCOPY clause will simply be ignored by the PL/SQL engine.

Important note: If an OUT or INOUT variable is passed by reference (NOCOPY) and the procedure terminates due to an unhandled exception (ends abnormally), the value of the referenced variable may no longer be valid.

Both stored procedures and functions are passed variables, the only difference is that a function can only be passed IN variables because a function returns a value.

Stored Procedures

A stored or named procedure is a module of code, stored in the database that can be called from another PL/SQL program. It is passed one or more variables and executes an action for the calling program. A procedure is created using the syntax below.

```
create or replace procedure <Name>
  (<variable list>)
as (or is)

  local variable declaration
begin
    code section
  exceptions
end;
```

The OR REPLACE clause allows the compiler to replace a procedure if a procedure of the same name is already in the database schema. This is handy during development so that you do not have to drop the procedure each time before recreating it.

The procedure can be called any valid object name. As with any database object, the procedure is created in the user's schema unless a schema name is provided. The example below creates the procedure in the PUBS schema. Of course, the user that creates the procedure must have rights granted to create objects in another schema.

```
create or replace procedure pubs.example_defaults
  (n_1 in number := 5,
   n_2 in number := 6,
   n_3 in number := 7)
as
begin
  dbms_output.put_line(n_1||n_2||n_3);
end;
/
```

The variable list is a comma delimited list of variables in the format:

```
name mode type := default
```

All of these items have been discussed above in the passing variables section above. The heading ends with the AS (or IS) clause. The heading takes the place of the DECLARE clause of the anonymous block. Local variables are declared between the AS and BEGIN key words. For clarity the developer may optionally want to append the procedure name to the END clause at the end of the procedure. As with all PL/SQL blocks, a procedure can contain an optional exceptions section (covered later in this Chapter).

When a procedure is sent to the database, it is compiled and stored in the database as an object. To execute the procedure you must call it.

```
SQL> create or replace procedure num_check
  2    (n_numb IN number)
  3  as
  4    v_line varchar2(40);
  5  begin
  6    if n_numb < 10
  7      then v_line:= 'Number OK';
  8    else
  9      v_line := 'Number Bad';
 10    end if;
```

```
11     dbms_output.put_line(v_line);
12   end num_check;
13   /

Procedure created.
```

The procedure heading is in lines 1, 2 and 3. One variable is passed into the procedure in IN mode and is internally named *n_numb*. A local variable called *v_line* is declared on line 4. Lines 5 through 12 define the procedure body. The procedure has been successfully compiled and loaded in the database. It has not been executed. Querying *user_objects* will show your procedures and their status.

```
SQL> set pages 999
SQL> column object_name format a30
SQL> select
  2    object_name,
  3    object_type,
  4    status
  5  from user_objects;

OBJECT_NAME                    OBJECT_TYPE         STATUS
------------------------------ ------------------- -------
AUTHOR                         TABLE               VALID
BOOK                           TABLE               VALID
BOOK_AUTHOR                    TABLE               VALID
EMP                            TABLE               VALID
EXAMPLE_DEFAULTS               PROCEDURE           INVALID
JOB                            TABLE               VALID
NUM_CHECK                      PROCEDURE           VALID
PUBLISHER                      TABLE               VALID
SALES                          TABLE               VALID
STORE                          TABLE               VALID

10 rows selected.
```

If the procedure did not compile correctly, it will still be loaded in the database but will be marked invalid as shown in the *example_defaults* procedure above. This invalid procedure was created earlier in the variable passing section.

```
SQL> create or replace procedure example_defaults
  2    (n_1 in number := 5,
  3     n_2 in number := 6,
  4     n_3 in number := 7)
  5  as
```

```
6  begin
7    n_1 := n_2 + n_3;
8  end;
9  /
```

Warning: Procedure created with compilation errors.

To see the compilation errors from SQL*Plus enter 'show errors';

SQL> show errors

Errors for PROCEDURE EXAMPLE_DEFAULTS:

```
LINE/COL ERROR
-------- ------------------------------------------------
7/3      PLS-00363: expression 'N_1' cannot be used as an assignment
target
```

To remove the procedure from the database, simply drop it.

```
SQL> drop procedure example_defaults;
```

Procedure dropped.

Once the procedure is in the database it can be called in a variety of ways using SQL*Plus, another PL/SQL block or from an external application connect to the database such as Java, Perl, etc.

Calling Procedures from SQL*Plus

To call a procedure from SQL*Plus use the execute command.

```
SQL> set serveroutput on
SQL> execute num_check(5);
Number OK
```

PL/SQL procedure successfully completed.

Because this procedure writes data to the buffer, SQL*Plus must be told to retrieve and display it. The SET SERVEROUTPUT ON command directs SQL*Plus to do this. The execute command runs the *num_check* procedure passing the literal number 5 as the IN variable. In order to execute a procedure from SQL*Plus that contains an OUT or INOUT variable, a

SQL*Plus variable must be created and used. In the example below, the procedure *get_area* is created and then executed being passed three variables. It then calculates the area and copies that value to the OUT variable *n_area*.

```
SQL> create or replace procedure get_area
  2    (n_length in number,
  3     n_width  in number,
  4     n_area   out number)
  5  as
  6  begin
  7    n_area := n_length*n_width;
  8  end get_area;
  9  /

Procedure created.

SQL> variable w_area number;
SQL> exec get_area(10,20,:w_area);

PL/SQL procedure successfully completed.

SQL> print w_area

    W_AREA
----------
       200
```

The variable *w_area* is the SQL*Plus variable. It is passed to the procedure by reference as indicated by the colon at the beginning of the variable name.

PL/SQL does not impose a limit on the number of variables that are passed into a procedure; however, the practical limit is based on user requirements. The more variables that are passed to a procedure, the harder it is to use and the more likely that the developer will cause errors. If the number of variables is too large, look at creating compound variables such as records, list or arrays. Passing five to six variables is about the practical limit. If the procedure is going to be overloaded in a package, that limit is reduced to 3 or 4 variables. Packages and overloading procedures is covered later in chapter 5 *Bulk Operations, Packages and Triggers.*

Calling Procedures from PL/SQL

I am so good at calling procedures; I do it all day long.

If calling a procedure from SQL*Plus is easy, calling it from PL/SQL is effortless. Simply call it in the code section of any PL/SQL block.

```
SQL> create or replace procedure get_area
  2     (n_length in number,
  3      n_width  in number,
  4      n_area   out number)
  5  as
  6  begin
  7    n_area := n_length*n_width;
  8  end get_area;
  9  /

Procedure created.

SQL> declare
  2     n_area number :=0;
  3  begin
  4    get_area(10,20,n_area);
  5    dbms_output.put_line('Area '||n_area);
  6  end;
  7  /

Area 200
```

Notice that the EXECUTE clause is not used. That is a SQL*Plus command and not used in PL/SQL. Also notice that the *n_area* variable is not passed by reference as in the SQL*Plus call. This is because the variable is local where as in the SQL*Plus example, it was external to the database.

The Return Clause with Procedures

As shown in the next section, a PL/SQL function is required to return a value using the RETURN clause. A procedure can also use the RETURN clause but can not return a value. Instead, the RETURN clause terminates execution of the procedure and processing passes back to the calling code. If the procedure was passed OUT or INOUT variables, the procedure will copy their values as of the RETURN clause. As with the GOTO clause, using the RETURN clause to terminate a procedure is considered bad programming practice and should be avoided.

PL/SQL Functions

A function is a PL/SQL named block that returns a value. It is commonly used to convert or assign values. Whereas a procedure is executed, a function is called, as in the example below:

```
Begin
   …
   get_area(10,20,n_area);
   n_area := calc_area(10,20);
   …
End;
```

In the code fragment above, the area is calculated by a procedure named *get_area* and a function names *calc_area*. The procedure was passed three values and it copied the calculated area into the *n_area* variable when the procedure exited. The next line uses a function that is passed two values, calculates the area, and returns that value, which is assigned to the *n_area* variable. Notice that the function is used directly in the assignment operation. A function is defined in the format below.

```
create or replace function <Name>
  (<variable list>) return <datatype>
as (or is)

  local variable declaration
begin
  code section
exceptions
end;
```

This is similar to the procedure definition except that it uses the return definition. A function returns a datatype, not a variable.

```
SQL> create or replace function calc_area
  2    (n_length in number,
  3     n_width  in number)
  4    return number
  5  as
  6  begin
  7    return n_length*n_width;
  8  end; /
Function created.
```

Above the function *calc_area* is defined so that it returns a number. In the function body there must be a RETURN statement defining what is returned. In the example above, the RETURN statement is in line 4.

A function name can be very descriptive with up to 32 characters and the function is always created in the schema of the user that creates the function. As with the procedure, a function can declare any number of values in the declaration section, limited only by the usability of the function. However, unlike a procedure, a function can not be passed variables in mode OUT or INOUT. A function can only return a datatype. If a function is defined with an OUT or INOUT variable, the function will compile but will raise an exception when executed.

```
ORA-06572: Function <name> has out arguments
```

An example used earlier in the book converted a temperature in Fahrenheit to Celsius. This is a perfect example of a function, which takes a value and returns a number.

```
SQL> create or replace function f2c
  2    (n_faren IN number)
  3    return number
  4  as
  5    n_cel number := 0;
  6  begin
  7    n_cel := (5/9)*(n_faren -32);
  8    return n_cel;
  9  end;
 10  /

Function created.
```

The function *f2c* takes a number in mode IN, calculates the values in Celsius and returns the Celsius value. If the function does not compile, SQL*Plus will display the errors with the "show errors" command.

```
SQL> create or replace function broken
  2    (n_faren IN number)
  3  as
  4    n_cel number := 0;
  5  begin
  6    n_cel := (5/9)*(n_faren -32);
  7    return n_cel;
  8  end;
  9  /

Warning: Function created with compilation errors.

SQL> show errors
Errors for FUNCTION BROKEN:

LINE/COL ERROR
-------- -------------------------------------------------
3/1      PLS-00103: Encountered the symbol "AS" when
expecting one of the following: return

5/1      PLS-00103: Encountered the symbol "BEGIN" when expecting
one of the following:  end function package
pragma private procedure subtype type use <an identifier>
<a double-quoted delimited-identifier> form current cursor
...
```

The function *broken* will not compile. Reading PL/SQL errors is a little different than reading errors in other programming languages. In PL/SQL, we focus with the top error. This is because most of the following errors will be caused by the first error. In this example, the first error states that the compiler found the AS key word when it expected something else, namely the RETURN clause. A look at the code shows that the function definition does not define a return datatype.

As with procedures, to find the function in the database, we query the *user_objects* view, as shown below.

```
SQL> set pages 999
SQL> column object_name format a30
SQL> select
  2     object_name,
  3     object_type,
  4     status
  5  from user_objects;

OBJECT_NAME                     OBJECT_TYPE          STATUS
------------------              -------------------  -------
AUTHOR                          TABLE                VALID
BOOK                            TABLE                VALID
BOOK_AUTHOR                     TABLE                VALID
BROKEN                          FUNCTION             INVALID
CALC_AREA                       FUNCTION             VALID
EMP                             TABLE                VALID
F2C                             FUNCTION             VALID
GET_AREA                        PROCEDURE            VALID
GET_AREA2                       PROCEDURE            VALID
JOB                             TABLE                VALID
NUM_CHECK                       PROCEDURE            VALID
PUBLISHER                       TABLE                VALID
SALES                           TABLE                VALID
STORE                           TABLE                VALID

14 rows selected.
```

To remove the function *broken* from the database, we can drop it with the "drop function" command.

```
SQL> drop function broken;

Function dropped.
```

RETURN Values in PL/SQL

As stated above, a function must return a value of the datatype defined in the header. The value can be a literal, a variable or a calculated value. The actual value returned is defined in the RETURN clause.

```
create or replace function full_name
  (v_fname IN author.author_first_name%type,
   v_lname IN author.author_last_name%type)
  return varchar2
as
begin
  return initcap(v_fname||' '||v_lname);
end;
/
```

The example above concatenates two variables and passes the result through Oracle's *initcap* function before returning the final results. A function can have multiple RETURN clauses but will terminate the function upon executing the first RETURN clause. In the example below, the CASE statement will insure that one of the four RETURN clauses is executed.

```
SQL> create or replace function num2word
  2    (n_number IN number)
  3    return varchar2
  4  as
  5  begin
  6    case n_number
  7      when 1 then return 'one';
  8      when 2 then return 'two';
  9      when 3 then return 'three';
 10    else return 'greater than 3';
 11    end case;
 12  end;
 13  /

Function created.

SQL> begin
  2    for i in 1 .. 4 loop
  3      dbms_output.put_line(num2word(i));
  4    end loop;
  5  end;
  6  /
one
two
```

```
three
greater than 3

PL/SQL procedure successfully completed.
```

If an IF/THEN statement is used, you may not reach a RETURN statement and the function will raise an exception.

```
SQL> create or replace function num2word
  2     (n_number IN number)
  3     return varchar2
  4   as
  5   begin
  6     if n_number = 1
  7       then return 'one';
  8     elsif n_number = 2 then return 'two';
  9     elsif n_number = 3 then return 'three';
 10     end if;
 11   end;
 12   /

Function created.

SQL> begin
  2     for i in 1 .. 4 loop
  3       dbms_output.put_line(num2word(i));
  4     end loop;
  5   end;
  6   /
one
two
three
begin
*
ERROR at line 1:
ORA-06503: PL/SQL: Function returned without value
ORA-06512: at "PUBS.NUM2WORD", line 9
ORA-06512: at line 3
```

Everything worked as expected except that when we passed a value greater than 3, the function ends without executing the RETURN clause. In this example, passing a too-high value causes the function to raise an exception. To avoid this error, we add a RETURN clause at the end of the function to catch any missed values. One of the most common causes of not executing a RETURN clause is due to the function raising an exception. If the function has an exception handling section (discussed next in this Chapter) the exception handler must contain a RETURN clause or it will simply raise another exception.

Remember, unlike a procedure, a function is never executed independently and it must be called to execute.

Calling PL/SQL Functions from SQL*Plus

To call a function in SQL*Plus, simply embed it in a SQL statement. Below we execute the *f2c* function by selecting it from the pseudo table called *dual*. The *"Dual"* pseudo-table allows you to select from it to execute functions.

```
SQL> select f2c(40) from dual;

   F2C(40)
----------
4.44444444
```

The function can be applied to any select statement that passed the correct datatype.

```
SQL> select f2c(quantity) from sales;

F2C(QUANTITY)
-------------
   537.777778
   -12.222222
   93.3333333
   204.444444
   426.666667
   82.2222222
   482.222222
...
   37.7777778
   4426.66667
   3037.77778
   4926.66667
   4871.11111
   37.7777778

100 rows selected.
```

The above example calculates the degrees Celsius from all the *quantity* values in the *sales* table (pretending that they are actually degrees Fahrenheit). For each row, the *f2c* function was executed, passing in the value of *quantity* for that row and returning that value converted to degrees Celsius.

Below is an example of a function that takes an author's first and last name and returns a formatted complete name. Notice that it used the *%type* definition for the passed in the variables.

```
SQL> create or replace function full_name
  2     (v_fname IN author.author_first_name%type,
  3      v_lname IN author.author_last_name%type)
  4     return varchar2
  5   as
  6   begin
  7     return initcap(v_fname||' '||v_lname);
  8   end;
  9   /

Function created.

SQL> select
  2     full_name(author_first_name, author_last_name) from author;

FULL_NAME(AUTHOR_FIRST_NAME,AUTHOR_LAST_NAME)
----------------------------------------------------
Mark Jones
Alvis Hester
Erin Weaton
Pierre Jeckle
Lester Withers
Juan Petty
Louis Clark
Minnie Mee
Dirk Shagger
Diego Smith
```

Calling Functions from PL/SQL

In a PL/SQL block, a function can be called in a SQL statement (as seen above) or used in a simple assignment operation.

```
SQL> declare
  2     v_far   number := &Farenheit;
  3     v_cels number := 0;
  4   begin
  5     v_cels := f2c(v_far);
  6     dbms_output.put_line(
             'Degrees Celcius is '|| f2c(v_far));
  7   end;
  8   /
```

```
Enter value for farenheit: 46

old   2:   v_far   number := &Farenheit;
new   2:   v_far   number := 46;

Degrees Celcius is 7.77777777777777777777777777777777777778
```

Functions can also be used to validate variables. In the example below the value of *n_test* is validated before additional processing.

```
SQL> create or replace function valid_numb
  2    (n_numb IN number)
  3    return boolean
  4  as
  5  begin
  6    if n_numb < 10 then return true;
  7    else return false;
  8    end if;
  9  end;
 10  /

Function created.

SQL> declare
  2    n_test number := &Test;
  3  begin
  4    if (valid_numb(n_test))
  5      then dbms_output.put_line('Valid');
  6    else dbms_output.put_line('Invalid');
  7    end if;
  8  end;
  9  /

Enter value for test: 8

old   2:   n_test number := &Test;
new   2:   n_test number := 8;

Valid

PL/SQL procedure successfully completed.

SQL> /

Enter value for test: 12

old   2:   n_test number := &Test;
new   2:   n_test number := 12;

Invalid

PL/SQL procedure successfully completed.
```

This is a simple test to determine if the number is less than 10. The function *valid_numb* returns a type Boolean, so it can be used as the condition of a comparison operation. Line 4 calls the function in order to get a true/false value which is used to control the program execution.

When should you use a procedure or a function? Since most modules can be written either as a procedure or a function, the decision between them comes down to efficiency and maintainability. Functions are preferred when a module returns one value. This value may be a variable, record or array, but as long as the module always returns one value, it is a good candidate for a procedure.

Local Modules

A local module is a procedure or function defined in the declaration section of another PL/SQL block. Because it is defined in a block, its scope is only in the block that defined it. The local module can not be called or executed by code outside of the defining block. The example below is an anonymous PL/SQL block that has a function defined in the declaration section.

```
SQL> declare
  2    v_test varchar2(40) := '&string';
  3
  4    function get_length
  5      (v_str IN varchar2)
  6      return number
  7    as
  8    begin
  9      return length(v_str);
 10    end;
 11  begin
 12    dbms_output.put_line(v_test||' has
              '||get_length(v_test)||' characters.');
 13  end;
 14  /
Enter value for string: Smitherdoodle
old   2:   v_test varchar2(40) := '&string';
new   2:   v_test varchar2(40) := 'Smitherdoodle';
```

```
Smitherdoodle has 13 characters.

PL/SQL procedure successfully completed.
```

The function *get_length* is defined in the anonymous block above and exist only within that block. There are a number of reasons to use local modules. First, by creating functions and procedures as local modules they are hidden from outside the defining block, allowing added functionality and code reuse while maintaining modularity. The local modules are hidden from other code within the containing package.

This protects object names and actions from code outside the defining block. Another benefit is that if used properly, local modules can make the code easier to read and maintain. However, these benefits can also be detractors. Local modules can not be used by code outside of the defining block, thereby limiting code reuse to only the defining block. Extensive use of local modules can lead to sections of code that perform the same functions located in multiple modules. This can result in lower code quality, maintainability and performance.

Retrieving the Source from the Database

The developers have created a set of procedures and functions and loaded them into the database. Sometimes you need to be able to pull the source code back out of the database. When a named block is sent to the database its source is loaded into the database and then compiled. The source is maintained in a view called *user_source*. To pull the source code out of the database, first list the objects in the database belonging to the user.

```
SQL> select
  2    object_name,
  3    object_type,
  4    status
  5  from user_objects;
```

```
OBJECT_NAME                     OBJECT_TYPE          STATUS
------------------------------  -------------------  ------
AUTHOR                          TABLE                VALID
BOOK                            TABLE                VALID
BOOK_AUTHOR                     TABLE                VALID
CALC_AREA                       FUNCTION             VALID
EMP                             TABLE                VALID
F2C                             FUNCTION             VALID
FULL_NAME                       FUNCTION             VALID
GET_AREA                        PROCEDURE            VALID
GET_AREA2                       PROCEDURE            VALID
JOB                             TABLE                VALID
MK_MONEY                        FUNCTION             VALID
NUM2WORD                        FUNCTION             VALID
NUM_CHECK                       PROCEDURE            VALID
PUBLISHER                       TABLE                VALID
SALES                           TABLE                VALID
STORE                           TABLE                VALID
VALID_NUMB                      FUNCTION             VALID

17 rows selected.
```

To find the code for the function *num2word* we look at *user_source*.

```
SQL> desc user_source;
 Name                           Type
 ----------------------------   -------------
 NAME                           VARCHAR2(30)
 TYPE                           VARCHAR2(12)
 LINE                           NUMBER
 TEXT                           VARCHAR2(4000)
```

The *user_source* view contains a row for each line of source code. To retrieve the code for the *num2word* function, select the text for that function.

```
SQL> select text
  2  from user_source
  3  where name = 'NUM2WORD'
  4  order by line;

TEXT
----------------------------------------
function num2word
  (n_number IN number)
  return varchar2
as
begin
  if n_number = 1
    then return 'one';
  elsif n_number = 2 then return 'two';
  elsif n_number = 3 then return 'three';
```

```
  end if;
end;
```

```
11 rows selected.
```

The code is listed in the format that it was submitted to the database. To find out which objects have source listed in *user_source*, select the object name.

```
SQL> select distinct name from user_source;

NAME
----------------------------
CALC_AREA
F2C
FULL_NAME
GET_AREA
GET_AREA2
MK_MONEY
NUM2WORD
NUM_CHECK
VALID_NUMB

9 rows selected.
```

The query must use the DISTINCT clause as there is a row for each line of source code defining each object. Since each line of source code is in a separate row in the view, you need to order the row by *line* or the lines could be returned out of order.

At this point, we have covered three of the four PL/SQL blocks; anonymous blocks, procedures and functions. The forth block, the trigger will be covered in Chapter 5 *Bulk Operations, Packages and Triggers*. Before continuing on to using PL/SQL to interact with the database, we need to cover PL/SQL's error handling capabilities. So what happens when PL/SQL runs into an error? If the error is caught during compilation, the PL/SQL compiler returns the error to the submitting application, such as SQL*Plus. If the code is already compiled and is executing in the database, the PL/SQL engine will raise an exception.

Exceptions in PL/SQL

Everyone Run!!!! The application just threw an exception!

Exceptions are like flags that are raised when a predefined event occurs, normally error conditions. Most programming languages "throw" exceptions but PL/SQL "raises" exceptions. Whether thrown or raised, the meaning is the same. When an exception is raised, program execution stops and jumps to the nearest exception handler. If the exception handler catches the exception, program execution resumes at the point right after the exception handler code.

Program execution never returns to the code that raised the exception unless the module is subsequently re-executed. If there is no exception handler in the module that raised the exception, execution returns to the calling block's exception handler. This continues until the exception is handled or the exception jumps out of the PL/SQL module and the exception is passed to the calling application (such as SQL*Plus or a script). Since none of the modules that we have presented so far have exception handlers, all exceptions are passed back to SQL*Plus which then

displayed the exception along with the error messages to the user.
Every PL/SQL block can have an optional exception handler.

```
SQL> declare
  2    n_1  number := 5;
  3    n_2  number := 0;
  4  begin
  5    n_1 := n_1/n_2;   -- divide by zero
  6    dbms_output.put_line(n_1);
  7  end;
  8  /
declare
*
ERROR at line 1:
ORA-01476: divisor is equal to zero
ORA-06512: at line 5
```

In the example above there is an exception raised because the
code tries to divide by zero. Since the block has no exception
handler, the exception is passed back to SQL*Plus to handle. An
exception handler or exception code is placed at the end of a
block before the END clause. If there is no exception raised, the
exception code is jumped and not executed.

```
begin
  ----- Code goes here
exception
  ----- Exception code goes here
end;
```

The exception code follows the format:

```
when <exception> then <handle code>;
when others then <handle code>;
```

The OTHERS option will catch all exceptions that are not
handled above the OTHERS clause. As with the CASE
statement, an exception will be handled by the first WHEN
clause that matches the exception, as show below.

```
SQL> declare
  2    n_1  number := 5;
  3    n_2  number := 0;
  4  begin
```

```
 5    n_1 := n_1/n_2;  -- divide by zero
 6    dbms_output.put_line(n_1);
 7  exception
 8    when ZERO_DIVIDE
 9      then dbms_output.put_line('You Divided By
             Zero');
10  end;
11  /

You Divided By Zero
```

Line 5 raises the exception when the division by zero occurs. Line 6 is jumped as the exception moves execution to the exception handler starting at line 7. Lines 8 and 9 actually handle the exception. Once the exception is handled, execution resumes at line 10, where the block ends.

As stated earlier, if an exception is not handled, it will fall through to the next higher or calling block's exception handler. This is shown in the example below where two functions are created, both with errors. The first will raise a CASE_NOT_FOUND exception on certain values. The second divides by zero.

```
SQL> create or replace function bad_convert
 2      (n_number IN number)
 3      return varchar2
 4  as
 5  begin
 6    case n_number
 7      when 1 then return 'one';
 8      when 2 then return 'two';
 9      when 3 then return 'three';
10    end case;
11  end;
12  /

Function created.

SQL> create or replace function divide_by_zero
 2      (n_1  IN  number)
 3      return number
 4  as
 5    n_2  number := 0;
 6  begin
 7    n_2 := n_1/n_2;  -- divide by zero
 8    return n_2;
 9  end;
10  /

Function created.
```

Neither of the functions above contains an exception handler. The PL/SQL block below will call these functions and cause an exception.

```
SQL> declare
  2    v_result varchar2(100);
  3    v_numb   number;
  4  begin
  5    -- buggy code, encase in a block
  6    begin
  7      for i in 1 .. 6 loop
  8        dbms_output.put_line(bad_convert(i));
  9      end loop;
 10    exception
 11      when INVALID_NUMBER
 12        then dbms_output.put_line('Invalid Number
             Exception');
 13      when ZERO_DIVIDE
 14        then dbms_output.put_line('Divide By Zero
             Exception');
 15    end;
 16
 17    -- more buggy code
 18    begin
 19      v_numb := divide_by_zero(25);
 20    end;
 21
 22  exception
 23    when others
 24      then dbms_output.put_line('Caught at the
             End');
 25  end;
 26  /

one
two
three
Caught at the End
```

The code begins to loop on line 7 but a CASE_NOT_FOUND exception is raised by the *bad_convert* function on line 8 when the loop index *i* equals 4. The exception is not handled in the function so the program execution instead jumps out of the function to the exception handler for the calling block which is line 10. This handler does not handle the CASE_NOT_FOUND exception so execution jumps to the outer block's exception handler at line 22.

This handler catches all exceptions with the OTHERS clause. Execution resumes at line 25 which is the end of the block. Notice that the procedure ended successfully. Since the exception was handled, SQL*Plus does not see the exception and instead sees the module end normally. The best place to handle the exception is normally in the offending block. A corrected version below now handles the exception.

```
SQL> create or replace function bad_convert
  2    (n_number IN number)
  3    return varchar2
  4  as
  5  begin
  6    case n_number
  7      when 1 then return 'one';
  8      when 2 then return 'two';
  9      when 3 then return 'three';
 10    end case;
 11  exception
 12    when CASE_NOT_FOUND
 13      then return 'Bad Conversion';
 14  end;
 15  /

Function created.

SQL> declare
  2    v_result varchar2(100);
  3    v_numb   number;
  4  begin
  5    -- buggy code, encase in a block
  6    begin
  7      for i in 1 .. 6 loop
  8        dbms_output.put_line(bad_convert(i));
  9      end loop;
 10    exception
 11      when INVALID_NUMBER
 12        then dbms_output.put_line('Invalid Number
            Exception');
 13      when ZERO_DIVIDE
 14        then dbms_output.put_line('Divide By Zero
            Exception');
 15    end;
 16
 17    -- more buggy code
 18    begin
 19      v_numb := divide_by_zero(25);
 20    end;
 21
 22    exception
```

```
 23      when others
 24        then dbms_output.put_line('Caught at the
               End');
 25  end;
 26  /

one
two
three
Bad Conversion
Bad Conversion
Bad Conversion
Caught at the End

PL/SQL procedure successfully completed.
```

The function *bad_conversion* now handles the exception and we can see this in the output above. But there is still an exception caused by the *divide_by_zero* function. The example below handles the divide by zero exception in the calling block.

```
SQL> declare
  2    v_result varchar2(100);
  3    v_numb   number;
  4  begin
  5    -- buggy code, encase in a block
  6    begin
  7      for i in 1 .. 6 loop
  8        dbms_output.put_line(bad_convert(i));
  9      end loop;
 10    end;
 11
 12    -- more buggy code
 13    begin
 14      v_numb := divide_by_zero(25);
 15    exception
 16      when INVALID_NUMBER
 17        then dbms_output.put_line('Invalid
               Number');
 18      when ZERO_DIVIDE
 19        then dbms_output.put_line('Divide By
               Zero');
 20    end;
 21
 22    exception
 23      when others
 24        then dbms_output.put_line('Caught at the
               End');
 25  end;
 26  /
```

```
one
two
three
Bad Conversion
Bad Conversion
Bad Conversion
Divide By Zero
```

The exception is handled in the calling block at line 18. The final exception routine is not executed as all exceptions are already handled. The block execution ends normally. Now that we know the basics, let's take a closer look at defining and raising exception in PL/SQL.

Defining and Raising Exceptions

Exceptions can be defined in the declaration section of any PL/SQL block. In fact, the exceptions discussed so far are Oracle-defined exceptions. By defining your own exceptions you can use the exception handling capability of PL/SQL to either act on errors, or terminate processing and return to the calling block. Below, two exceptions are defined in the declaration section of an anonymous PL/SQL block.

```
declare
  creditcard_no_good exception;
  creditcard_overlimit exception;

begin
  -- customer places items in cart
  if (check_out) then
    begin
      get_customer_data(n_custNum, ... );
      if (creditcard) then
        begin
          if (invalid) then raise
                    creditcard_no_good;
          if (overLimit) then raise
                    creditcard_overlimit;
        end;
    exception
      when creditcard_no_good then ...
      when creditcard_overlimit then ...
      when others then raise big_problem;
    end;
  ... more processing
end;
```

Two exceptions are defined in the declaration section of the above code fragment. During customer checkout, the customer credit card is verified and if it fails, the exceptions are raised, and the exception handler catches both exceptions and handles them. Any other exception is handled by the OTHERS clause which itself raised a BIG_PROBLEM exception (handled somewhere else in the code). The code can also raise an Oracle defined exception. Below, the function catches the CASE_NOT_FOUND exception and raises the ZERO_DIVIDE exception.

```
SQL> create or replace function bad_convert
  2     (n_number IN number)
  3     return varchar2
  4  as
  5  begin
  6    case n_number
  7      when 1 then return 'one';
  8      when 2 then return 'two';
  9      when 3 then raise ZERO_DIVIDE;
 10    end case;
 11  exception
 12    when CASE_NOT_FOUND
 13      then return 'Bad Conversion';
 14  end;
 15  /

Function created.
```

Programmer defined exceptions should be named so that the user (or maintainer) understands what raised the exception. The BIG_PROBLEM exception is an example of a poorly named exception. It is not very informative to have your application fail with a BIG_PROBLEM exception because it is ambiguous. Oracle provides the RAISE_APPLICATION_ERROR procedure to allow the programmer to provide additional information to an exception definition when the exception is raised.

RAISE_APPLICATION_ERROR

The RAISE_APPLICATION_ERROR is actually a procedure defined by Oracle that allows the developer to raise an exception and associate an error number and message with the procedure. This allows the application to raise application errors rather than just Oracle errors. Error numbers are defined between -20,000 and -20,999. All other numbers belong to Oracle for its own errors. The message can be anything that will fit in a varchar2(2000). The final parameter passed to the procedure is a Boolean (true/false) that tells the procedure to add this error to the error stack or replace all errors in the stack with this error. Passing the value of 'True' adds the error to the current stack, while the default is 'False'.

```
SQL> create or replace procedure test_var
  2     (n_test   IN   number := 0,
  3      n_result OUT number)
  4   as
  5   begin
  6     if n_test > 100 then
  7        raise_application_error(-20010,'Number Too
           Large');
  8     end if;
  9     n_result := n_test;
 10   end;
 11   /

Procedure created.

SQL> declare
  2     n_numb number := &Number;
  3     n_2 number := 0;
  4   begin
  5     test_var(n_numb, n_2);
  6     dbms_output.put_line(n_2);
  7   end;
  8   /
Enter value for number: 5
old   2:   n_numb number := &Number;
new   2:   n_numb number := 5;
5

PL/SQL procedure successfully completed.

SQL> /
Enter value for number: 105
old   2:   n_numb number := &Number;
```

```
new    2:    n_numb number := 105;
declare
*
ERROR at line 1:
ORA-20010: Number Too Large
ORA-06512: at "PUBS.TEST_VAR", line 7
ORA-06512: at line 5
```

The number value over 100 resulted in the exception being raised and SQL*Plus displayed the error number and message. The RAISE_APPLICATION_ERROR will also populate the SQL errors codes so that they can be programmatically handled.

SQLCODE and SQLERRM

Oracle provides a way to capture the error codes when a SQL statement raises an exception by using the SQLCODE and SQLERRM globally-defined variables. Both SQLCODE and SQLERRM can be useful in tracking exceptions that are handled by the OTHERS clause of the exception handler. SQLCODE returns the current error code from the error stack. SQLERRM returns the error message from the current error code as shown below.

```
SQL> declare
  2     n_numb number := &Number;
  3     n_2 number := 0;
  4  begin
  5     test_var(n_numb, n_2);
  6     dbms_output.put_line(n_2);
  7  exception
  8     when others then
  9       begin
 10         dbms_output.put_line('SQLCODE: '||SQLCODE);
 11         dbms_output.put_line('Message: '||SQLERRM);
 12       end;
 13  end;
 14  /
Enter value for number: 105
old    2:    n_numb number := &Number;
new    2:    n_numb number := 105;
SQLCODE: -20010
Message: ORA-20010: Number Too Large
```

Using the same function from the previous example, a value greater than 100 will raise an exception. The OTHERS clause in the exception handler caught the exception and printed out the SQLCODE and SQLERRM. Once you know the error code, you can programmatically handle the exception, like this:

```
SQL> declare
  2    n_numb number := &Number;
  3    n_2 number := 0;
  4  begin
  5    test_var(n_numb, n_2);
  6    dbms_output.put_line(n_2);
  7  exception
  8    when others then
  9      begin
 10        if SQLCODE = -20010
 11          then dbms_output.put_line('Value Too
                 Large');
 12        else dbms_output.put_line('Unknown
                 Exception');
 13        end if;
 14      end;
 15  end;
 16  /

Enter value for number: 105

old   2:   n_numb number := &Number;
new   2:   n_numb number := 105;

Value Too Large
```

Handling exceptions is an important programming practice that is all too often overlooked. Many times, exception handling is added too late, after the code is written and deployed, or when the developer is attempting to stop or locate programming errors. Exception handling should be a part of the program design and should be included in all appropriate PL/SQL blocks. Properly raising and handling exceptions will allow the developer to effectively track and maintain the code. The ability to programmatically recover from system, application, and user errors is important in keeping the application running and the users happy.

Conclusion

This Chapter covered creating and using PL/SQL procedures and functions. We started with a discussion on passing variables, then covered procedures and functions, and finally ended by introducing exceptions and exception handling.

If a function or procedure is going to perform meaningful work, they must have access to variables. Variables passed to procedures and functions are defined in the heading section as unconstrained types. Each passed variable has a mode of either IN, OUT or INOUT. Variables of mode IN are read-only and cannot be receivers of an assignment operation. Instead, IN operators are normally passed by reference.

Variables of mode OUT are write-only. They are created but not initialized until they are initialized within the procedure. When the procedure ends the value is copied to the variables that were passed from the calling program. Variables of type INOUT can be read and written. If a procedure raised an unhandled exception, the OUT and INOUT variables will not have values copied to the passed variables.

Unnamed variables are assigned in the order they are passed from left to right. If variables are not passed in order, they must be named to identify the corresponding procedure variable.

A stored procedure is a module of code stored in the database that can be called from another PL/SQL block. It is passed one or more variables and performs some action for the calling code. Stored procedures are executed in SQL*Plus by using the EXECUTE command. In PL/SQL a stored procedure is simply called by the executing block.

A function is also a module of code stored in the database and functions are called from inside a SQL statement or used in an assignment. Functions are passed zero or more variables and always return a single value. A function can not be passed variables of mode OUT or INOUT.

Exceptions are flags raised when errors occur. They can be raised by the system, the database or the application. When an exception is raised program execution halts and transfers to the exception handler for that block. If there is no exception handler defined or the handler does not handle that exception, the exception is passed to the outer or calling block's exception handler.

This continues until the exception is either handled or the exception is passed out of the program to the calling application such as SQL*Plus. If an exception is handled, program execution resumes below the handler that handled the exception.

At this point we have covered the programmatic basics of PL/SQL. It is now time to integrate PL/SQL with SQL so that the application can interact with the database. The next Chapter is devoted to the SELECT INTO statement and PL/SQL cursors.

Using SQL and Cursors

Using SQL and Cursors

So far we have focused on the programmatic part of PL/SQL, how to define and use variables, controlling program flow, and catching program exceptions. These are all important topics, but all programming languages implement these capabilities. The capability that really sets PL/SQL apart from other languages is its ability to interact with the data in the database.

This chapter will focus on retrieving and manipulating data from Oracle and we will discuss retrieving, inserting and updating data. We start with the SELECT INTO query which is used to retrieve one and only one row of data from the database.

The SELECT INTO Clause

The SELECT INTO clause of SQL is used to retrieve one row or set of columns from the Oracle database. The SELECT INTO is actually a standard SQL query where the INTO clause is used to place the returned data into predefined variables.

```
SQL> declare
  2    v_authName author.author_last_name%type;
  3  begin
  4    select
  5      author_last_name into v_authName
  6    from
  7      author
  8    where
  9      author_key = 'A103';
 10
 11    dbms_output.put_line('Name: '||v_authName);
```

```
12  end;
13  /
```

Name: weaton

Here the *author_key* was used to retrieve one author's last name and place it in the variable called *v_authName*. The query can also retrieve an entire row as a record.

In the example below a record based on the columns of the *author* table is declared in line two below. Because *v_author* is declared as an author table *%rowtype*, you can safely use the SELECT * clause to retrieve all the columns.

```
SQL> declare
  2     v_author author%rowtype;
  3  begin
  4     select
  5       * into v_author
  6     from
  7       author
  8     where
  9       author_key = 'A103';
 10
 11     dbms_output.put_line('Name:
                 '||v_author.author_first_name||' '||
                   v_author.author_last_name);
 12  end;
 13  /

Name: erin weaton
```

If the DBA adds a column to the *author* table, the query above will still execute. The record variable *v_author* contains a record that includes all the columns in the *author* table. If the value of a column in the table is NULL, it will also be NULL in the record. The individual columns are accessed using the dot "." notation.

You can see this in line 11 of the listing. Although it is important to define variables using the database datatype definition of the retrieved data, sometime this is not possible.

This is shown in the example below.

```
SQL> declare
  2     v_totalName varchar2(80);
  3  begin
  4    select
  5      initcap(author_last_name||',
                      '||author_first_name)
          into v_totalName
  6    from
  7      author
  8    where
  9      author_key = 'A105';
 10    dbms_output.put_line('Name: '||
        v_totalName);
 11  end;
 12  /

Name: Withers, Lester
```

The query above is returning a string value created from multiple table columns. The variable *v_totalname* must be defined as a datatype that can hold the composite string returned by the query. If the SELECT INTO clause attempts to load a value into a variable that is the wrong datatype, or not large enough to contain the value, an exception is raised.

Although a SELECT INTO can only return one row of data, it can return multiple columns into multiple variables. In the example below, two columns are selected from a table and loaded into two predefined variables.

```
SQL> declare
  2     v_lname author.author_last_name%type;
  3     v_fname author.author_first_name%type;
  4  begin
  5    select
  6      author_first_name, author_last_name
  7      into v_fname, v_lname
  8    from
  9      author
 10    where author_key = 'A108';
 11
 12    dbms_output.put_line('Name: '||v_fname||'
'||v_lname);
 13  end;
 14  /

Name: minnie mee
```

A single row of column values is loaded into the list of variables when multiple columns are selected. The order of the columns and the order of the variables must match.

In each example so far, the restriction defined in the query's WHERE clause has been based on a primary key. Using a unique or primary key is important as the SELECT INTO clause can not retrieve more that one row of data. If the query returns more that one row an exception is thrown.

```
SQL> declare
  2    v_authName author.author_last_name%type;
  3  begin
  4    select
  5      author_last_name into v_authName
  6    from
  7      author
  8    where
  9      author_state = 'MO';
 10    dbms_output.put_line('Name: '||v_authName);
 11  end;
 12  /

declare
*
ERROR at line 1:
ORA-01422: exact fetch returns more than requested number of rows
ORA-06512: at line 4
```

The above example retrieved the authors from the *author* table with an *author_state* of 'Missouri'. There are three authors in the author table from Missouri and the SELECT INTO raised a TOO_MANY_ROWS exception.

Another issue with using SELECT INTO statement is that it throws an exception is it fails to return at least one rows.

```
SQL> declare
  2    v_authName author.author_last_name%type;
  3  begin
  4    select
  5      author_last_name into v_authName
  6    from
```

```
 7       author
 8     where
 9       author_state = 'FL';
10     dbms_output.put_line('Name: '||v_authName);
11   end;
12   /
declare
*
ERROR at line 1:
ORA-01403: no data found
ORA-06512: at line 4
```

Here the query asks for authors from Florida. Since there are not any authors in the table from Florida, the SELECT INTO raises a NO_DATA_FOUND exception. Your PL/SQL code should be written in such a way that it is able to handle these exceptions. Anytime the SELECT INTO raises an exception, the query will not load a value into the defined variable.

When you try and access the variable, you will either get another exception or worse, use an old or invalid variable value. So using the SELECT INTO query can be problematic. However since a SELECT INTO query can return one and only one row of data, it makes a perfect PL/SQL function. Within the function, your code can catch and handle the possible exceptions.

Below is an example of wrapping the SELECT INTO query in a function with exception handling.

```
SQL> create or replace function auth_Name
  2    ( v_auth_state IN author.author_state%type)
  3    return varchar2
  4  as
  5    v_authName author.author_last_name%type;
  6  begin
  7    select
  8      author_last_name into v_authName
  9    from
 10      author
 11    where
 12      author_state = v_auth_state;
 13    return v_authName;
 14    exception
 15    when TOO_MANY_ROWS
 16      then return 'Too Many Authors in that
                      State';
 17    when NO_DATA_FOUND
```

```
18        then return 'No Authors in that State';
19    when others
20        then raise_application_error(
21        -20011,'Unknown Exception in authName
                Function');
22  end;
23  /

Function created.
```

Notice when the function code catches an exception it must handle it and return something appropriate or pass the exception back to the calling block. In the above example, the code catches and handles the TOO_MANY_ROWS and NO_DATA_FOUND exception, which should cover most of the exceptions the function will encounter.

However, if an unexpected exception is raised, the function code raises an application error on line 20. As shown below, the function will provide an appropriate return value when used.

```
SQL> select auth_Name('MO') from dual;

AUTH_NAME('MO')
-------------------------------------------
Too Many Authors in that State

SQL> select auth_Name('CO') from dual;

AUTH_NAME('CO')
-------------------------------------------
No Authors in that State

SQL> select auth_Name('CA') from dual;

AUTH_NAME('CA')
-------------------------------------------
jeckle

SQL> select auth_Name('KY') from dual;

AUTH_NAME('KY')
-------------------------------------------
mee

SQL> select auth_Name('12345') from dual;

AUTH_NAME('12345')
-------------------------------------------
No Authors in that State
```

As the last example showed, even if an invalid state value is passed to the function, the internal query will raise an exception and the function will handle it and return an appropriate value indicating no authors were found.

There are a number of SQL attributes that are also available for use with the SELECT INTO query; however the attributes are not as useful when used in PL/SQL code. Below is a list of the attributes.

- SQL%NOTFOUND - True if no rows returned.

- SQL%FOUND - True if one or more rows returned

- SQL%ISOPEN - True if the SQL cursor is open.

- SQL%ROWCOUNT - Number of rows returned.

Why are these attributes less useful in PL/SQL? Because of PL/SQL's ability to raise and handle exceptions, you already know an attribute's value before you test the attribute. The code fragment below creates a function that uses the *sql%found* attribute.

```
SQL> create or replace function auth_Name
  2    ( v_auth_state IN author.author_state%type)
  3    return varchar2
  4  as
  5    v_authName author.author_last_name%type;
  6  begin
  7    select
  8      author_last_name into v_authName
  9    from
 10      author
 11    where
 12      author_state = v_auth_state;
 13    if SQL%FOUND then return v_authName;
 14    end if;
 15  end;
 16  /

Function created.
```

The function compiles and runs returning the results below. The function uses the sql%found attribute to test that the query returned a values before the function returns. The example below uses the function.

```
SQL> select auth_Name('CA') from dual;

AUTH_NAME('CA')
------------------------------------
jeckle
```

What is the issue with using the *sql%found* attribute on line 13? Remember, the SELECT INTO throws an exception if no data is returned. Therefore, the attribute check at line 13 is unnecessary because if *sql%found* was false, the query would have already raise an exception and would not executed line 13. Here is an annotated example of the previous function that implements exception handling.

```
SQL> create or replace function auth_Name
  2    ( v_auth_state IN author.author_state%type)
  3    return varchar2
  4  as
  5    v_authName author.author_last_name%type;
  6  begin
  7    select
  8      author_last_name into v_authName
  9    from
 10      author
 11    where
 12      author_state = v_auth_state;
 13    if SQL%FOUND then return v_authName;
 14    end if;
 15    exception
 16    when TOO_MANY_ROWS
 17      then
 18          return 'Authors Found: '||SQL%ROWCOUNT;
 19    when NO_DATA_FOUND
 20      then
 21  if SQL%NOTFOUND then return 'No Authors in
                               that State';
 22        end if;
 23    when others
 24      then raise_application_error(
 25        -20011,'Unknown Exception in authName
                Function');
 26  end;
 27  /

Function created.
```

We already know line 13 is redundant, but so is line 21. The only way line 21 is executed is if the SELECT INTO query returned no rows and thus *sql%notfound* would equal true. But you already know that sql%notfound is true because the statement is contained in the NO_DATA_FOUND exception handler. We do not need the condition test in lines 13 or 21 because we already know the results. Notice that the exception handle catches the TOO_MANY_ROWS exception and returns the number of rows found in line 18. This appears to be logical, but the example below shows that the handle does not return the number of rows.

```
SQL> select auth_Name('MO') from dual;

AUTH_NAME('MO')
--------------------------------------
Authors Found: 1
```

Since we know from a previous example that there are three authors from Missouri, why did *sql%rowcount* return only one? When the query returned the second row, the TOO_MANY_ROWs exception was raised.

As a result of the raising the exception, *sql%rowcount* will operate as you would expect. The attribute *sql%rowcount* will return zero (0) if the query returned no rows, (but the NO_DATA_FOUND exception is raised) and a one (1), if one or more rows were returned. As the example shows, using the *sql%rowcount* attribute with a SELECT INTO query does not provide any new information about the query's execution.

The attribute *sql%isopen* is used to check that the implicit cursor used by the database has been closed. Since the database opens and closes the cursor used by the query, any test of the attribute will result in a false.

So to recap, if *sql%found* is true, the query did note raise an exception, so why check it. If the attribute *sql%notfound* is true, the NO_DATA_FOUND exception has already been raised so the only place to check the attribute value is in the exception handler, which your code would not be executing if data was found.

The *sql%isopen* attribute will always be false, because the database opens and closes the implicit cursor used to retrieve the data. And finally, the attribute *sql%rowcount* equals 0 if no rows were found (but the exception is raised) and a 1, if one or more rows are found (if more than one an exception is raised).

The one place you can use some of these attributes is inside an exception handler, as shown in the example below.

```
SQL> create or replace function auth_Name
  2    ( v_auth_state IN author.author_state%type)
  3    return varchar2
  4  as
  5    v_authName author.author_last_name%type;
  6  begin
  7    select
  8      author_last_name into v_authName
  9    from
 10      author
 11    where
 12      author_state = v_auth_state;
 13    return v_authName;
 14    exception
 15    when others
 16      then
 17        if SQL%NOTFOUND then return 'No Authors
            in that State';
 18        elsif SQL%FOUND then return 'Too Many
            Authors in that State';
 19        else raise_application_error(
 20        -20011,'Unknown Exception in authName
              Function');
 21        end if;
 22  end;
 23  /

Function created.
```

```
SQL> select auth_Name('CA') from dual;

AUTH_NAME('CA')
-------------------------
jeckle

SQL> select auth_Name('MO') from dual;

AUTH_NAME('MO')
-------------------------
Too Many Authors in that State

SQL> select auth_Name('FL') from dual;

AUTH_NAME('FL')
-------------------------
No Authors in that State
```

In the example above, all the exceptions are caught by the
OTHERS clause and handled internally using the
IF/THEN/ELSE statement. The code produces the same
results as the original example.

So, which coding method is better? The best choice is the one
that is clearest to the programmers that have to create and
maintain the code. Many times an exception handler will handle
some exceptions and use the OTHERS clause to raise exceptions
based on the SQL attributes and the SQLERR codes.

But what do we do if we know that our query will return zero or
more rows and we want to process each of the rows returned? In
this case you must use a cursor to retrieve and process however
many rows the query returns.

PL/SQL Cursors

A cursor is used to retrieve and process zero or more rows of
data. There are a number of steps to use a cursor and depending
on how you implement the cursor, you can control each step or
have the database perform them. A cursor is based on a
SELECT statement, normally declared in the declaration section

of a PL/SQL block. The statement is not restricted as to the columns retrieved or number of tables joined.

Any valid SQL statement can be used to implement a cursor. Cursors are used to retrieve and process data. There is no cursor for inserts, updates or deletes. In the following set of examples we will step through the process of defining and using cursors. In the example function *my_func*, a cursor named *c1* is defined in the function's declaration section.

```
create or replace function my_func
  return number
as

  cursor c1 is
    select store_name, sum(quantity) qty
    from store join sales using (store_key)
    group by store_name;
```

In this example, the cursor *c1* joins the *store* and *sales* tables. Since we are going place the rows in a record, the column *sum(quantity)* must be aliased to a valid column name. If all the columns are going to be returned, you can use the SELECT * clause like this:

```
cursor c2 is select * from author;
```

Normally a cursor definition determines what data will be retrieved by the cursor. However, sometime a cursor is defined as a variable that can return different columns based on how it is later used. These cursors can include the RETURNING clause to define the columns that the cursor will return.

```
cursor c3 returning book%rowtype;
```

Using cursors with a RETURNING clause will be discussed further in the discussions of REF CURSORS.

Once declared, the cursor can be used in your code. To use a cursor you must first open it. When a cursor is opened, the SQL statement is executed and the table rows involved in the query is identified by the database. The database's consistent view mechanism will ensure that all data retrieved by the cursor is consistent as of the moment the cursor is opened. The database will maintain this consistent view until the cursor is closed. For this reason, it is important to close the cursor as soon as processing permits.

```
open c1;
```

A cursor must be closed to release the database resources it is holding. As long as the cursor is open, the database must maintain the consistent view.

```
close c1;
```

Once the cursor is closed, it again becomes a definition. One important note is that exceptions thrown while processing a cursor can jump pass the CLOSE statement. It is important to ensure that the cursor is closed in the exception handling routine if exceptions are raised.

If you attempt to open a cursor that is already open, the cursor will raise an exception. Likewise, if you attempt to close a cursor that is not open, the cursor will raise an exception. Since you need to insure that the cursor is closed, use the cursor attribute *%isopen* to test the cursor's state before attempting to close the cursor. Below is a code fragment of an exception handler that tests a cursor's state and closes the cursor if open. We will discuss all of the cursor attributes in the next section.

```
exception
  when others then
    if c1%isopen then close c1;
    end if;
end;
```

The exception handler tests the cursor's state before closing it.

When a cursor is opened, the rows of data are not retrieved by the database. The actual rows must be retrieved, one at a time using the FETCH clause. Before you can fetch a row, you must create a variable to hold the returned data.

As with the SELECT INTO query, there are two options for defining these variables: separate variables for each returned column, or use a record based on the cursor row *%type*. Using the example cursor *c1* defined earlier, the first example defines separate variables for each column.

```
cursor c1 is
    select
      store_name,
      sum(quantity) qty
    from
      store
      join
      sales using (store_key)
    group by
      store_name;

st_name store.store_name%type;
total   number;

begin
  open c1;
  fetch c1 into st_name, total;
```

The cursor fetch returns two values and they are placed in the defined variables. As with the SELECT INTO query, the order of the columns and the list of variables in your PL/SQL code must match. If the cursor returns a large number of values or if the number of values may change, it is better to create the variable as a cursor *%rowtype*.

```
cursor c1 is
    select
      store_name,
      sum(quantity) qty
    from
      store
```

```
    join
    sales using (store_key)
  group by
    store_name;

r_c1 c1%rowtype;

begin
  open c1;
  fetch c1 into r_c1;
```

Each time a fetch is executed the next row of data is returned. Cursor rows are accessed in the order that they are returned. If you require data from a row that has already been processed, you must close the cursor, reopen it and reprocess the data to the required row.

When the last row is fetched, all subsequent fetches will return the last row. We need a way to get information about the cursor state so that we can determine when the last row has been fetched. Oracle provides cursor attributes to allow you to determine the cursor's state.

PL/SQL Cursor Attributes

Oracle provides four attributes to get information about the state of a cursor.

```
cursor%found
```

Returns true if the last fetch returned a new row. Before the first fetch, *%found* is null. After the first fetch, (if it returned a new row) *%found* is true. After the first fetch that does not return a new row, *%found* is false.

```
cursor%notfound
```

Returns true if the last fetch does not return a new row. The *%notfound* is basically the opposite of the *%found* attribute.

```
cursor%rowcount
```

Returns the number of rows that have already been fetched. Before the first row, *%rowcount* is zero. As each row is fetched, *%rowcount* increases by one.

```
cursor%isopen
```

Returns true if the cursor is currently open. Before the cursor is opened and after the cursor is closed, it returns false.

Note: all the attributes except *cursor%isopen* will throw an exception if called before the cursor is opened or after the cursor is closed.

So we have the basics for creating, testing and using a cursor, it is time to put cursors to work.

Using PL/SQL Cursors

A cursor requires a set of steps in order to be used. These steps are as follows:

1. Define the cursor.

2. Open the cursor

3. Process all the rows in a loop.

    a. Fetch a row.

    b. Check that a new row was returned.

    c. Process the row, return to set 4.

    d. End the loop.

4. Close the cursor.

The cursor is defined in the declaration section of the PL/SQL block. We will see later that some cursors can also be defined in

---

the procedural code. The cursor is then opened, which causes the database to establish a consistent view. Normally in a loop, the rows are then fetched into a variable or record. In PL/SQL, you normally will test to ensure that new rows were returned by the fetch before processing the row. If a new row was not returned, the loop is terminated. Once all the rows have been processed, the cursor is closed to release all the cursor's database resources. The next example demonstrates each step in using a cursor.

```
SQL> create or replace function max_store
  2    return varchar2
  3  as
  4    cursor c1 is
  5      select
  6        store_name, sum(quantity) qty
  7      from store join sales using (store_key)
  8      group by store_name;
  9
 10    r_c1 c1%rowtype;
 11    largest number := 0;
 12    lg_name store.store_name%type;
 13  begin
 14    open c1;
 15    loop
 16      fetch c1 into r_c1;
 17      exit when c1%notfound;
 18      if r_c1.qty > largest then
 19        largest := r_c1.qty;
 20        lg_name := r_c1.store_name;
 21      end if;
 22    end loop;
 23    close c1;
 24
 25    return ('Highest Sales is: '||
 26          lg_name||'   '||largest);
 27  end;
 28  /

Function created.

SQL> select max_store from dual;

MAX_STORE
------------------------------------------------

Highest Sales is: hot wet and sexy books   24700
```

The cursor *c1* is defined on lines 4 through 8. Line 10 defines a record to hold a row of fetched data. To ensure robustness in the function, the record is defined as a *c1%rowtype*. As with table *%rowtype*, the record will contain each of the columns in the cursor definition, and they will be the same datatype as the underlying columns in the database. The cursor is opened on line 14.

Once line 14 is executed, the database will maintain a consistent view for the entire life of the cursor. Lines 15-22 define the loop that is used to process the rows. Line 16 fetches a row of data and places it into the record variable *r_c1*. Line 17 checks the *%notfound* attribute to ensure that a new row was fetched.

If the fetch did not return a new row, then *%notfound* will be true and the loop will exit. Lines 18-20 process the data in the record. Once the loop exits (the fetch does not return a new row), line 23 closes the cursor, freeing all the database resources.

The programmer can also use the while loop to process a cursor, but must insure that one fetch takes place before the condition test at the start of the loop.

```
SQL> declare
  2     cursor c2 is
  3        select initcap(author_last_name)
           from author;
  4    l_name author.author_last_name%type;
  5    begin
  6      open c2;
  7      fetch c2 into l_name;
  8      while c2%found loop
  9        dbms_output.put_line(l_name);
 10        fetch c2 into l_name;
 11      end loop;
 12      close c2;
 13    end;
 14    /
```

```
Jones
Hester
...
Smith

PL/SQL procedure successfully completed.
```

In the above example, the cursor returns only one column and it is fetched into a variable rather than a record. The variable is defined on line 4. Line 7 executes the initial fetch. This must happen before starting the while loop to initialize the *c2%found* attribute. The WHILE loop will fetch a new row of data at the bottom of the loop on line 10 allowing the condition test to occur before processing the new row.

A cursor can be used to determine the average quantity of all the orders in the *sales* table. Of course to find the average you can use the *avg* function but this example is demonstrating using the cursor *%rowcount* attribute.

```
SQL> declare
  2    cursor c3 is
  3      select quantity from sales;
  4    n_c3    number;  -- holds cursor value
  5    average number := 0;
  6    counter number := 0;
  7  begin
  8    open c3;
  9    loop
 10      fetch c3 into n_c3;
 11      exit when c3%notfound;
 12      average := average + n_c3;
 13    end loop;
 14    counter := c3%rowcount;
 15    close c3;
 16    dbms_output.put_line('Average Quantity = '||
 17                          average/counter);
 18  end;
 19  /

Average Quantity = 1105.5
```

The average sales value is the sum of all the quantities in the *sales* table, divided by the number of orders (or rows). The variable *average* was used to sum all the quantities. Line 14 assigned the value of the cursor *%rowcount* attribute to the variable *counter*. Notice that the assignment was executed before closing the cursor. Once the cursor is closed, *c3%rowcount* becomes undefined.

The previous examples have fetched into a cursor *%rowtype* and into variables. If the cursor returns multiple values, it can fetch them into multiple variables in the same manner as the SELECT INTO query. In the example below, the cursor selects three columns into three variables. The block lists the stores that have above average sales. First it must find the average sales, then the code list the stores with sales above average. Notice that the cursor is opened and processed twice. As stated, to reprocess a cursor result set, it must be closed and reopened.

```
SQL> declare
  2    cursor c4 is
  3      select store_name, store_key,
            sum(quantity) as qty
  4      from store join sales using (store_key)
  5      group by store_name, store_key;
  6
  7    v_name   store.store_name%type;
  8    v_key    store.store_key%type;
  9    n_qty    number := 0;
 10    sumer    number := 0;
 11    average number := 0;
 12  begin
 13    open c4;
 14    loop
 15      fetch c4 into v_name, v_key, n_qty;
 16      exit when c4%notfound;
 17      sumer := sumer + n_qty;
 18    end loop;
 19    average := sumer/c4%rowcount;
 20    close c4;
 21
 22    dbms_output.put_line(
            'Average Store Sales: '||average);
 23    open c4;
 24    loop
 25      fetch c4 into v_name, v_key, n_qty;
 26      exit when c4%notfound;
 27      if average < n_qty then
 28        dbms_output.put_line(initcap(v_name)||',
 29                            '||v_key||', '||n_qty);
 30      end if;
```

```
31    end loop;
32    close c4;
33 end; /

Average Store Sales: 11055
Hot Wet And Sexy Books, S107, 24700
Eaton Books, S109, 12120
Wee Bee Books, S104, 13700
Borders, S102, 21860
Books For Dummies, S105, 13000
```

The cursor fetch placed the returned column values in the variables *v_name*, *v_key*, and *n_qty*. The example opened, processed, and closed the cursor twice. The first time, the only value used was *qty* and as such, the example cursor was poorly implemented. A real cursor should never bring back unused data. The code should have defined a second cursor that only returned the *qty* column.

Cursors can also be nested. The example below uses two cursors to list authors and the books they have sold.

```
SQL> declare
 2    cursor c5 is
 3      select initcap(author_last_name) a_name,
 4        author_key
 5      from author;
 6    cursor c6 is
 7      select initcap(book_title) bk_title,
 8          sum(quantity) sales, author_key
 9      from
10        book join sales using (book_key)
11            join book_author using (book_key)
12      group by initcap(book_title), author_key;
13    r_c5 c5%rowtype;
14    r_c6 c6%rowtype;
15  begin
16    open c5;
17    loop
18      fetch c5 into r_c5;
19      exit when c5%notfound;
20      dbms_output.put_line(chr(10)||
        r_c5.a_name);
21      begin
22        open c6;
23        loop
24          fetch c6 into r_c6;
25          exit when c6%notfound;
26      if r_c5.author_key = r_c6.author_key then
```

```
27        dbms_output.put_line (r_c6.bk_title||
28                          ', '||r_c6.sales);
29          end if;
30        end loop;
31        close c6;
32      end;
33    end loop;
34    close c5;
35  end;
36  /
```

```
Jones
Windows Success, 18200

Hester
Windows Success, 18200
Pay No Taxes And Go To Jail, 16400
Oracle9i Sql Tuning, 1100

Weaton
Unix For Experts, 1400
Piano Greats, 16290
Reduce Spending The Republican Way, 2750

… Results truncated for brevity
```

The outer cursor (*c5*) is efficient, returning only those columns needed. The inner cursor (*c6*) however brings back all the book information for all authors each time it is opened. If the database contained thousands of books, this block would be very inefficient. What is needed is a way to make the inner cursor (*c6*) return only those rows belonging to the specific author. This can be achieved by passing the cursor a variable or parameter.

Passing Parameter to PL/SQL Cursors

A cursor is passed a parameter in very much the same way a procedure is passed a parameter except that the parameter can only be IN mode. Like the procedure, the cursor definition will declare an unconstrained datatype for the passed variable.

```
cursor c7 (v_key varchar2) is
    select initcap(book_title) bk_title,
        sum(quantity) sales, author_key
    from
      book join sales using (book_key)
          join book_author using (book_key)
```

```
          where author_key = v_key
          group by initcap(book_title), author_key;
```

The cursor above is defined as accepting a parameter with a datatype of *varchar2*. In this example, the variable is used in the WHERE clause to filter the results before grouping. By substituting cursor c7 for c6 in the above example, the PL/SQL block becomes much more efficient because the inner cursor returns only the row belonging to the specified author.

```
SQL> declare
  2    cursor c5 is
  3      select initcap(author_last_name) a_name,
  4        author_key
  5      from author;
  6    cursor c7 (v_key varchar2) is
  7      select initcap(book_title) bk_title,
  8          sum(quantity) sales, author_key
  9      from
 10        book join sales using (book_key)
 11            join book_author using (book_key)
 12      where author_key = v_key
 13      group by initcap(book_title), author_key;
 14    r_c5 c5%rowtype;
 15    r_c7 c7%rowtype;
 16  begin
 17    open c5;
 18    loop
 19      fetch c5 into r_c5;
 20      exit when c5%notfound;
 21      dbms_output.put_line(chr(10)||
                                    r_c5.a_name);
 22      begin
 23        open c7(r_c5.author_key);
 24        loop
 25          fetch c7 into r_c7;
 26          exit when c7%notfound;
 27          dbms_output.put_line (r_c7.bk_title||
 28                          ', '||r_c7.sales);
 29        end loop;
 30        close c7;
 31      end;
 32    end loop;
 33    close c5;
 34  end;
 35  /
```

The results returned in this example are the same as the previous example and to save space were omitted. This example using *c7* is much more efficient than using *c6* because it eliminated returning unneeded data in cursor *c7* and also allows the removal of the IF/THEN clause with its condition test. Notice line 23 opened the cursor and passed the current *author_key* from the outer cursor. If line 23 did not pass in the parameter when the cursor was opened, PL/SQL would throw an exception.

```
    open c7;
    *
ERROR at line 23:
ORA-06550: line 23, column 7:
PLS-00306: wrong number or types of arguments in
   call to 'C7'
ORA-06550: line 23, column 7:
PL/SQL: SQL Statement ignored
```

Let's close with one final note about cursors. This example was used to demonstrate nested cursors and passing parameters to cursors. Even though the final version was far more efficient that the first version, it still violates an important rule of PL/SQL programming, do not execute SQL inside a loop unless there is no other way to get the data.

The example could have been written to execute one cursor that returned all the needed data: *author_name*, *book_title*, and *sales*. And then it could have use a loop to process the results. This method would be even more efficient as it would execute only one query against the database. So far we have manually controlled the cursor and there is many times when you want that level of control. However, Oracle has provided a streamlined method of using cursors with a *FOR* loop.

PL/SQL Cursor For Loop

In the previous section we learned that a sequence of steps is followed to define and use a cursor.

1. Open the cursor.

2. Start a loop.

3. Fetch a row of data.

4. Check for a new row, exit if not.

5. Process the data.

6. End the loop.

7. Close the cursor.

Since these steps are almost always followed, Oracle provides a way to let PL/SQL perform most of the steps. This is called the CURSOR FOR loop. As in the name, it uses a FOR loop to process the cursor.

```
SQL> declare
  2    cursor c8 is
  3      select
  4        initcap(author_last_name)  l_name,
  5        initcap(author_first_name) f_name
  6      from author;
  7  begin
  8    for r_c8 in c8 loop
  9      dbms_output.put_line(r_c8.f_name||' '||
 10                          r_c8.l_name);
 11    end loop;
 12  end; /

Mark Jones
Alvis Hester
Erin Weaton
Pierre Jeckle
Lester Withers
Juan Petty
Louis Clark
Minnie Mee
Dirk Shagger
Diego Smith
```

The CURSOR FOR is a very efficient cursor. Lines 2 through 6 define the cursor. Line 8 handles opening the cursor, fetching the rows, testing for new rows, and exiting when a new row is not returned. Notice that the record *r_c8* is not defined in the declaration section. The CURSOR FOR automatically defines *r_c8* as a *c8%rowtype*. The scope for *r_c8* is only inside the

CURSOR FOR loop. Likewise, the cursor attributes for cursor *c8* are defined only inside the CURSOR FOR loop.

If you define the record *r_c8* in the declare section of the PL/SQL block, the variable you defined will go out of scope when the CURSOR FOR defines the record *r_c8* and will return in scope when the loop ends. If there is a requirement to access the cursor attributes from outside the loop, a variable must be defined and the cursor attribute copied into it before the loop ends. The CURSOR FOR closes the cursor at the END LOOP clause. Below is an example that calculates the average of total store sales by store, using the cursor *%rowcount* attribute.

```
SQL> declare
  2     cursor c9 is
  3       select sum(quantity) qty
  4       from sales group by store_key;
  5     sumer    number := 0;
  6     counter number := 0;
  7  begin
  8     for r_c9 in c9 loop
  9       sumer := sumer + r_c9.qty;
 10       counter := c9%rowcount;
 11     end loop;
 12     dbms_output.put_line('Average is '||
 13           sumer/counter);
 14  exception
 15     when others then
 16       if c9%isopen then close c9;
 17       end if;
 18  end; /

Average is 11055
```

In order to count the number of items summed, the attribute *c9%rowcount* must be assigned inside the loop at line 10. Also note that an exception happening inside the loop will jump to the exceptions handler which must ensure that the cursor is properly closed.

The CURSOR FOR can also be passed parameters. It follows the same rules as the manual cursor in that if the cursor is defined with a parameter, it must be opened with a parameter, or the cursor will raise an exception.

```
SQL> declare
  2    cursor c10(v_avg in number) is
  3      select store_name, sum(quantity) qty
  4      from store join sales using (store_key)
  5      group by store_name
  6      having sum(quantity) > v_avg;
  7  begin
  8    for r_c10 in c10 (11055) loop
  9      dbms_output.put_line(initcap(
 10          r_c10.store_name)||
              '            '||r_c10.qty);
 11    end loop;
 12  end; /

Borders                     21860
Books For Dummies           13000
Hot Wet And Sexy Books      24700
Wee Bee Books               13700
Eaton Books                 12120
```

The variable *v_avg* is defined as an IN parameter. This designation is optional as a variable can only be passed as mode IN, and the passed parameter can also be assigned a default value. If a default value is assigned, then the cursor can be opened without passing a parameter and it will use the defined default value.

Notice in the example below that *v_avg* is assigned a default value in line 2, and the cursor is opened without passing a parameter in line 8.

```
SQL> declare
  2    cursor c10(v_avg number:= 11055) is
  3      select store_name, sum(quantity) qty
  4      from store join sales using (store_key)
  5      group by store_name
  6      having sum(quantity) > v_avg;
  7  begin
  8    for r_c10 in c10 loop
  9      dbms_output.put_line(initcap(
 10          r_c10.store_name)||
              '            '||r_c10.qty);
 11    end loop;
 12  end;
 13  /
```

```
Borders                 21860
Books For Dummies       13000
Hot Wet And Sexy Books  24700
Wee Bee Books           13700
Eaton Books             12120
```

Another nice feature of the CURSOR FOR is the ability to define the cursor inline. Below is a cursor that is not declared in the declaration section of the executing block. The cursor definition is included in the CURSOR FOR.

```
SQL> begin
  2    for r_c11 in
       (select author_last_name l_name,
  3            author_first_name f_name
  4                    from author) loop
  5      dbms_output.put_line(initcap(
  6        r_c11.l_name||
           ', '||r_c11.f_name));
  7    end loop;
  8  end;
  9  /

Jones, Mark
Hester, Alvis
Weaton, Erin
Jeckle, Pierre
Withers, Lester
Petty, Juan
Clark, Louis
Mee, Minnie
Shagger, Dirk
Smith, Diego
```

Defining a cursor inline has the advantage of self documenting the cursor in the code. Instead of going back to the declare section to determine the cursor definition, the programmer maintaining the code can see the definition right there in the code that calls it.

However, if the cursor is used multiple times, it will be in multiple locations in the code, reducing maintainability.

Another problem with defining the cursor inline is that the cursor will have no defined name. Therefore you will not be able to access the cursor attributes. This can be a problem if an exception is raised inside the cursor that jumps out of the loop.

You can get around this problem by wrapping the loop inner statements in a separate block with an exception handler.

```
begin
  for r_c11 in (select author_last_name l_name,
                       author_first_name f_name
                from author) loop
    begin
      dbms_output.put_line(initcap(r_c11.l_name||
                           ', '||r_c11.f_name));
      -- lots of other stuff to do.
    exception
      when others then
        -- handle all exceptions
    end;
  end loop;
end;
```

The exception handler must deal with all the exceptions without raising new ones unless it terminates the program. Any exception raised in the exception handler will jump to the end of the loop and leave the cursor open.

Another powerful feature of the CURSOR FOR is the update feature. This allows the programmer to efficiently update data returned by the cursor.

Cursor For Update

A SELECT statement is a read only operation to the database and the Oracle database never blocks a read. Even if there are locks on rows, the database will allow a statement to read those rows (subject to the requirement to maintain a consistent view). Locks are placed on rows when they have been changed and a commit/rollback has not yet ended the transaction. Until the user changing the row has ended the transaction, the lock remains and no other user can make changes to the locked data.

Normally, you update, insert, or delete information using standard SQL statements.

```
begin
  insert into store
     values (select * from pubs.new_store);
end;
```

Sometimes you will want to select and lock the data so that you restrict anyone else from making changes to the data until you are finished. To retrieve and lock the data we use the CURSOR FOR UPDATE syntax.

The example below has a lot of new PL/SQL constructs for us to examine. The function of this code is to update the *quantity* column in the *sales* table for every order for *store_key* 'S101'. Let's just say the author bribed us to increase his sales record.

```
SQL> declare
  2     cursor c12 is
  3        select store_key
  4        from sales
  5        for update of quantity;
  6  begin
  7    for r_c12 in c12 loop
  8      if r_c12.store_key = 'S101' then
  9         update sales
 10         set quantity= quantity+1
 11         where current of c12;
 12      end if;
 13    end loop;
 14  end;
 15  /
```

The cursor is declared using the FOR UPDATE clause and the *quantity* column is identified as the item that will be updated. At line 7 the database opens the cursor which locks all the rows in the *sales* table. An IF/THEN statement is used to identify the rows (*orders*) that belong to the store with 'S101' as it's key. Those rows are then updated in lines 9 through 11.

Notice that lines 9 through 11 are actually one line of code. The UPDATE WHERE CURRENT OF clause automatically updates the row that the cursor is currently using at that time. Because the update SQL does not have to relocate the row to update, it is very fast. At the end of the PL/SQL block, all the rows selected by the cursor are still locked (not just the changed rows). The transaction stays open and the locks are held until a rollback or commit is issued.

Notice that cursor *c12* locks all the rows in the *sales* table because it will update the *quantity* column. This cursor could have been defined as the cursor below with the same effect.

```
declare
  cursor c12 is
    select store_key
    from sales
    for update;
begin
```

If the cursor will join tables, then all the rows returned by the cursor in both tables are locked.

```
declare
  cursor c12 is
    select author_last_name, book_title
    from author join book_author using (author_key)
                join book        using (book_key)
    for update;
begin
```

Here the cursor locks all the rows in the *author* table, the *book_author* table and the *book* table. This is because the cursor returns all the rows in each of the three tables. If the intent is to update the *book_title* column in the *book* table, the cursor can indicate that as shown in the example below.

```
declare
  cursor c12 is
    select author_last_name
    from author join book_author using (author_key)
                join book        using (book_key)
```

```
        for update of book_title;
begin
```

Now the database will only lock the rows in the *book* table because the cursor indicates that although it will retrieve more data, it will only update the *book* table. This is an important point. The database will keep all the rows locked until the transaction ends, not the cursor is closed. As the programmer, you want to lock as little data in the database as possible. Always specify the columns to update in the cursor definition to reduce unnecessary row locking.

Here are some important points to remember about the FOR UPDATE clause:

- Lock as few rows as possible. Locks reduce concurrency and cause waits, slowing-down your processing.

- Even though the cursor indicates that it is going to change some data, it is not required to change any values.

- Even if the cursor identifies a column to update (such as *book_title* in the above example) it can still update other columns or tables. In this case, the updates may be blocked by locks held by other users.

- The locks remain until the end of the transaction (Commit or Rollback), not the closing of the cursor.

- If another transaction has locks on the data, the cursor open will wait (block) on those locks. There is no restriction on the time the cursor will wait for the locks to be released. The NOWAIT clause can be appended to the cursor definition to tell it to return immediately (without opening the cursor) if there are already locks on the data.

- The WHERE CURRENT OF clause can be used for updates or deletes. It does not make sense to insert a row at the current cursor location.

- The CURSOR FOR UPDATE using the WHERE CURRENT OF clause is the fastest way to update data. The cursor will use the *rowid* to perform the update (or delete) which is the fastest way to locate a specific row in an Oracle database table.

Cursors can also be defined as variables. These variables are known as REF CURSORS because the variable references the actual cursor.

PL/SQL Ref Cursors

A ref cursor is a variable, defined as a cursor type, which will point to, or reference a cursor result. The advantage that a ref cursor has over a plain cursor is that is can be passed as a variable to a procedure or a function. The REF CURSOR can be assigned to other REF CURSOR variables. This is a powerful capability in that the cursor can be opened, then passed to another block for processing, then returned to the original block to be closed. The cursor variable can also be returned by a function and assigned to another variable. The REF CURSOR variable is not a cursor, but a variable that points to a cursor. Before assigning a cursor variable, a cursor type must be defined.

```
type author_cursor is ref cursor;
```

This REF CURSOR is a weak typed cursor variable because it does not define the datatype the cursor will return. Below is the same cursor that is strongly typed.

```
type author_cursor is ref cursor
      returning author%rowtype;
```

By strongly typing the cursor variable, you define what the cursor can return. If a strongly typed cursor returns something other that its return type, a ROWTYPE_MISMATCH exception is raised. A strongly typed cursor type is less flexible but less prone to programming errors. The PL/SQL compiler will verify that the FETCH clause has the correct variable/record for the cursor return type at compile time.

Once the cursor type is defined, the actual variable can be defined as the cursor type.

```
c1 author_cursor;
```

Now *c1* is a variable of a cursor type. It is opened using a SQL statement.

```
open c1 for select * from authors;
```

Now *c1* has all the attributes of the actual cursor. As with any cursor it is important to close the cursor as soon as you have completed processing.

```
SQL> declare
  2    type auth_cursor is ref cursor;
  3    c1 auth_cursor;
  4    r_c1 author%rowtype;
  5  begin
  6    open c1 for select * from author;
  7    fetch c1 into r_c1;
  8      if c1%isopen then
  9        dbms_output.put_line(
                        'The Cursor is open.');
 10      end if;
 11      dbms_output.put_line(
                    'Row Count is '||c1%rowcount);
 12    close c1;
 13    if not c1%isopen then
 14     dbms_output.put_line(
                        'The Cursor is closed.');
 15    end if;
 16  end;
 17  /

The Cursor is open.
Row Count is 1
The Cursor is closed.
```

Here some of the cursor attributes are used to process the cursor. Notice that the record used to hold a fetched cursor row is defined as an *author* table *%rowtype*. Even though the example cursor variable is defined, the record can not use it because the cursor variable return type is not defined. The example below attempts to create a cursor *%rowtype* variable for processing.

```
SQL> declare
  2     type auth_cursor is ref cursor;
  3     c1 auth_cursor;
  4     r_c1 c1%rowtype;
  5  begin
  6     null;
  7  end;
  8  /
   r_c1 c1%rowtype;
        *

ERROR at line 4:
ORA-06550: line 4, column 8:
PLS-00320: the declaration of the type of this
expression is incomplete or malformed
ORA-06550: line 4, column 8:
PL/SQL: Item ignored
```

I hate it when I'm Malformed!!!

However, a strongly typed cursor can use the cursor variable to define the cursor record.

```
SQL> declare
  2     type auth_cursor is ref cursor
return author%rowtype;
  3     c1 auth_cursor;
  4     r_c1 c1%rowtype;
  5   begin
  6     null;
  7   end;
  8   /
```

In this example, the *auth_cursor* type returns an *author%rowtype*. Because this is defined in line 2, the record defined in line 4 can now use it.

Cursor variables that are weakly typed can be defined to return any values. In the example below, the cursor variable *c1* is defined as three different statements.

```
SQL> declare
  2     type auth_cursor is ref cursor;
  3     c1 auth_cursor;
  4     r_c1   author%rowtype;
  5     r2_c1 book%rowtype;
  6     r3_c1 number;
  7   begin
  8     open c1 for select * from author;
  9       fetch c1 into r_c1;
 10     close c1;
 11     open c1 for select * from book;
 12       fetch c1 into r2_c1;
 13     close c1;
 14     open c1 for select sum(quantity)
 15             from store join sales
                   using (store_key)
 16             group by store_name;
 17       fetch c1 into r3_c1;
 18     close c1;
 19   end;
 20   /
```

Although the block does not do anything but open and close the cursor variable, it does demonstrate that weakly typed variables can be defined differently each time the variable is opened. But what happens when a cursor variable is defined with a SQL statement but returns unexpected values? Below is an example of defining a cursor variable of one type and the record as another.

The cursor variable is returning all columns in the *book* table, but the receiving variable is defined as a record of columns from the *author* table.

```
SQL> declare
  2     type auth_cursor is ref cursor;
  3     c1 auth_cursor;
  4     r_c1   author%rowtype;
  5   begin
  6     open c1 for select * from book;
  7        fetch c1 into r_c1;
  8     close c1;
  9   end;
 10   /
declare
*
ERROR at line 1:
ORA-06504: PL/SQL: Return types of Result Set
variables or query do not match
ORA-06512: at line 7
```

Notice that the error message is pointing to the DECLARE clause. That is because the block successfully compiled and only threw the error when it was executed. The PL/SQL compiler can not catch the error because the cursor type did not define a return type. By changing the definition of the cursor type to a strongly typed definition, the compiler will catch this error when the code is compiled.

```
SQL> declare
  2     type auth_cursor is ref cursor
  3          return book%rowtype;
  4     c1 auth_cursor;
  5     r_c1   author%rowtype;
  6   begin
  7     open c1 for select * from book;
  8        fetch c1 into r_c1;
  9     close c1;
 10   end;
 11   /

   fetch c1 into r_c1;
     *
ERROR at line 8:
ORA-06550: line 8, column 5:
PLS-00394: wrong number of values in the INTO
list of a FETCH statement
ORA-06550: line 8, column 5:
PL/SQL: SQL Statement ignored
```

Now the compiler catches the error. So far the examples have been using the cursor variables as regular cursors. The real advantage of using a cursor variable is the ability to pass it as a parameter. In the example below a local function is used to open a cursor called *c1* and return it.

The block body calls the function to assign the cursor to the cursor variable *c2*. The block body then processes the cursor and closes it.

```
SQL> declare
  2     type auth_cursor is ref cursor
return author%rowtype;
  3     c2 auth_cursor;
  4     r_c2 c2%rowtype;
  5
  6     function get_auth return auth_cursor
  7     is
  8       c1 auth_cursor;
  9     begin
 10       open c1 for select * from author;
 11       return c1;
 12     end;
 13
 14  begin
 15     c2 := get_auth;
 16     loop
 17       fetch c2 into r_c2;
 18       exit when c2%notfound;
 19       dbms_output.put_line(initcap(
r_c2.author_last_name));
 20     end loop;
 21     close c2;
 22  end;
 23  /

Jones
Hester
Weaton
Jeckle
Withers
Petty
Clark
Mee
Shagger
Smith
```

Line 2 defines the cursor type. Lines 3 and 4 define the cursor and return record used in the body. Line 6 declares a local function called *get_auth* that returns an *auth_cursor* type. Inside this local function, cursor *c1* is defined as an *auth_cursor* type, opened and returned to the calling code. The function is actually executed on line 15 when *c2* is assigned the return value of the *get_auth* function. The cursor *c2* is processed and finally closed on line 21. Note that *c1* opened the cursor and *c2* closed it. This is an important point. The example contains only **ONE** cursor. When *c2* is assign the value of *c1*, both variables point to the same cursor. Remember that *c1* and *c2* are variables that point to or reference the actual cursor.

The same basic example is shown below except, the output is generated by a local procedure. Note that the procedure *print_name* gets passed the cursor *c2* and then processes it. It then passes the cursor backup to be closed by the body of the PL/SQL block.

```
SQL> declare
  2    type auth_cursor is ref cursor
return author%rowtype;
  3    c2 auth_cursor;
  4    r_c2 c2%rowtype;
  5
  6    function get_auth return auth_cursor
  7    is
  8      c1 auth_cursor;
  9    begin
 10      open c1 for select * from author;
 11      return c1;
 12    end;
 13
 14    procedure print_name (c3 in out auth_cursor)
 15    as
 16      r_c3 author%rowtype;
 17    begin
 18      loop
 19        fetch c3 into r_c3;
 20        exit when c3%notfound;
 21        dbms_output.put_line(
           initcap(r_c3.author_last_name));
 22      end loop;
 23    end;
 24
```

```
25  begin
26    c2 := get_auth;
27    print_name(c2);
28    close c2;
29  end;
30  /


Jones
Hester
Weaton
Jeckle
Withers
Petty
Clark
Mee
Shagger
Smith
```

There are three items you should note about this PL/SQL block. First, the body is pretty simple to understand. Get the authors, print the names, and close the cursor. Second, you can pass cursor variables to procedures and functions, and functions can return the variables. Lastly, it can become confusing about when a cursor variable should be closed.

In Chapter 5 *Bulk Operations, Packages and Triggers*, you will be introduced to packages where REF CURSORS can be shared by any code local to the package.

Conclusion

This Chapter focused on using PL/SQL to interact with data in the database. We covered both retrieving data and manipulating it. Starting with the SELECT INTO and then moving to the many types and variations of cursors. It demonstrated multiple ways to manipulate the data in the database.

The SELECT INTO query is used to retrieve one and only one row of data. If it returns more that one row of data then a TOO_MANY_ROWS exception is raised. If no data is returned, a NO_DATA_FOUND exception is raised. A variable, set of variables, or a record must be defined to accept the data row retrieved. Because the SELECT INTO query returns one, and only one row, it is a good candidate to be wrapped in a function. The function can internally catch and handle any exception thrown.

Cursors are used when the number of returned rows can be zero or more. Cursors do not throw exceptions based on the number of rows returned. Cursors have attributes that allow you to determine the cursor's current state. The only attribute defined when the cursor is not open is the cursor *%isopen* attribute. To use a cursor it must be declared, opened, each row fetched, and then closed. This is normally done in a loop. The CURSOR FOR uses a FOR loop to execute all of the steps needed to process a cursor.

Cursors should be defined in a manner that retrieves only the data needed to process. To make cursors more efficient, you can pass parameters to the cursor when they are opened. Cursors should be closed as soon as processing is completed to free the cursor's database resources.

The CURSOR FOR UPDATE will lock all the defined rows when it is opened. It should only be used when you need to keep other users from modifying the data retrieved by the cursor, until cursor processing is completed. Closing the cursor will not release the database locks, only a commit or rollback will release the locks created by the CURSOR FOR UPDATE.

Cursor variables or REF CURSORS are variables that point to cursors. The advantage of the cursor variable is that it can be passed to procedures and functions, or assigned to other cursor variables of the same type. Cursor variables must still be closed and are often closed in a different routine than the one that opened them.

The next Chapter will introduce some of PL/SQL's more advanced features. These include bulk operation on large amounts of data, collections, packages, and database triggers.

Bulk Operations, Packages and Triggers

Collections are my specialty!

Bulk Operations, Packages and Triggers

This chapter will wrap up our discussion of with PL/SQL advanced capabilities, including collections, bulk SQL operations, PL/SQL packages, and database triggers. These are some of PL/SQL's most powerful capabilities.

PL/SQL collections provide the developer with the ability to load sets of objects into RAM memory where the data can be manipulated with great speed. Processing data in a PL/SQL collection does not have the overhead of constantly retrieving and manipulating data in the database, and collections also form the basis for allowing PL/SQL to execute bulk operations.

Bulk operations include retrieving large amounts of data from the database and manipulating large amounts of data in the database, via operations such as bulk inserts, bulk update and bulk deletes. Using bulk operations instead of single line fetches can provide a significant performance boost when dealing with large sets of data.

Encapsulating code into PL/SQL packages is one of the most important capabilities in PL/SQL, but sadly, many developers do not implement them. Packages allow PL/SQL blocks to persist and share data and code, and packages also allow for procedure and function overloading. The database also handles code in PL/SQL packages more efficiently by bringing the entire package into memory. All PL/SQL development (other than trivial programs) should be designed and implemented within PL/SQL packages.

Our final PL/SQL subject will be triggers. Triggers allow the developer to execute PL/SQL code based on "events" that happen within the database. A trigger is tied to a database event and when that event happens, the trigger will execute the defined code. Triggers can be used to implement database auditing, log database changes or capture and store server errors. Triggers can also archive data by saving deleted data into history tables. In sum, triggers are a very powerful database feature.

So why did all these important subjects get lumped into the final Chapter? It is because you needed to understand PL/SQL basics before any of these functions can be implemented. You can not bulk collect data if you can't processes the data. You can't share data in a package until you can create procedures and functions to process data. All of these advanced capabilities continue to build on the PL/SQL basics that we covered in earlier chapters.

Before a developer can bulk collect data into memory, he/she must be able to create a structure to store it. This memory structure is called a collection. Let's take a closer look.

PL/SQL Collections

A collection is a group of objects that are stored in memory for processing. The first type of collection that most programmers learn about is a linked list; however, there are many other types of collections. Programming languages such as Visual Basic, Java and C++ have a rich set of tools to work with collections. This is because when using a programming language, all objects being manipulated are in memory. If a developer is working with more than a few objects, a collection becomes an efficient and convenient way to hold objects in memory, where they can be processes hundreds of time faster than if they were on disk storage.

Oracle has provided collections in PL/SQL since Oracle8 but many PL/SQL developers do not use collections. This is mostly due to the fact that the PL/SQL developer has something the Java/C++ developer does not, the Oracle database. Storing objects in the database (even in global temporary tables) incurs a lot of overhead for the disk I/O. The PL/SQL developer can attain a significant performance improvement by using collections to hold and manipulate objects in memory rather than continually inserting and retrieving them from the database.

Oracle's PL/SQL collections allow the PL/SQL programmer to place a set of objects in one defined variable (the collection). This collection variable can be passed from one procedure to another. Collection variables are homogenous, meaning that all the objects in a PL/SQL collection must be of the same data type. Oracle provides three types of collections: PL/SQL tables, nested tables, and VARRAYs. The nested table and the

VARRAY can be stored in the database table as a column datatype. The PL/SQL table is a memory only structure.

Before creating a collection the collection type must be defined. Once the collection type is defined, a variable is defined as that collection type.

```
declare
  type auth_var is varray(1000) of author%rowtype;
  type authnme_var is varray(300) of
                      author.auth_last_name%type;

  a_auth auth_var;
  a_aname authnme_var;

begin
```

The example above defines two VARRAY types. One contains an *author* table row type, and the other contains an *author last name* column type. To use a collection you must be able to determine information about the collection. Oracle provides several methods to access and manipulate collections. Let's take a closer look at collection methods.

PL/SQL Collection Methods

Before discussing creating and using collection, we need to introduce the methods used to obtain information about a collection. These methods are like the SQL attributes except that instead of variables, they are actually functions that return information. The methods are accessed using the dot notation from a defined collection. After we introduce the methods, we will demonstrate each of them using them with the three collection types.

COUNT

COUNT returns the number of valid objects in the collection, not the size of the collection. Sparse collections can contain deleted elements so the size of the collection and the number of objects can be different.

```
n_numb = a_auth.count;
```

The number of objects in the *a_auth* VARRAY is stored in the *n_numb* variable. COUNT will return 0 for an empty collection. If the COUNT method is used on a nested table or VARRAY before it is initialized, a COLLECTION_IS_NULL exception is raised.

FIRST

The FIRST method returns the index of the first element in the array (or the lowest index in the collection). It does not return the value of the element.

```
n_numb = a_auth.first;
```

The variable *n_numb* now contains the index of the first element in the collection.

LAST

The LAST method is like the FIRST method except that is returns the index of the last element (or the highest index value) in the collection.

```
n_numb = a_auth.last;
```

LIMIT

The LIMIT method returns the defined limit for a VARRAY. The VARRAY is the only collection with a defined limit. The LIMIT method can be used to verify that you can add additional elements to the array without exceeding the array's defined size.

```
if a_auth.last < a_auth.limit then ....
```

Here we verify that the index of the last element is less than the defined array limit.

PRIOR

One of the advantages of using a collection over using a cursor is that you can move both forward and backward through the collection. The PRIOR method takes an index and returns the index of the next earlier (or lower) valid element.

```
n_numb = auth.prior(a_auth.last);
```

Here we assign the index of the second to the last valid element to the variable *n_numb*. So why not use index - 1 to find the previous element? The element preceding the current element may not be valid, and accessing it could result in an exception being raised. If the PRIOR method is executed on the first element, it will return the index to the first element, so it can not be used exclusively to walk the collection.

```
n_numb1 = auth.prior(a_auth.first);
n_numb  = a_auth.first;
```

Here both variables will equal the *a_auth.first* index.

NEXT

The NEXT method is the same as the prior method except that it returns the index of the next valid element.

```
n_numb = auth.next(a_auth.first);
```

As with the PRIOR method, using the NEXT method after the last element will return the last element's index. You can not use the NEXT method to determine that you are at the end of the collections.

DELETE and TRIM

DELETE and TRIM are covered together because they both remove elements from a collection. Using the DELETE method without an argument removes all the elements in a collection. The DELETE method with arguments removes only the specified elements.

```
auth.delete;     -- removes all elements.
auth.delete(4); -- removes the fourth element
auth.delete(4,8);- removes all elements from 4 to 8
                 - inclusive.
```

When you delete an element, the element is removed from the collection, however the location in the collection still exists and you can place a new element into the collection at that location. If the element you delete does not exist, the DELETE method will return back to the calling code, having done nothing. It's also important to note that no PL/SQL exception is raised when you delete a non-existing element.

The TRIM method removes elements only from the end of a collection. Without an argument, the TRIM method removes the last element.

```
auth.trim;     -- removes the last elements.
auth.trim(4); -- removes the last four element
```

If you try to trim more elements than exist, the TRIM that executes after the first element is removed will raise a SUBSCRIPT_BEYOND_COUNT exception.

Now the warning! Do not mix the TRIM and DELETE methods on the same collection. Remember that the DELETE

---

method removes the element and keeps the location so you can reuse it again. The TRIM method removes the element and the location. If you deleted the last element using the DELETE method, the element location will remain. If you subsequently use the TRIM method to remove the next element, the TRIM method will actually remove the empty place left by the DELETE method and the actual last element will remain intact.

EXIST

If I am going to manually work through a collection that contains deleted elements, I must be able to determine if the collection element is valid, this is the function of the EXIST method. The EXIST method returns a true or false, but never a null. It returns a true if the element location contains a valid element, otherwise it returns a false.

You can not determine the last element of a collection with the EXIST method because if you test an element past the last element, the EXIST method will simply return false. You can not determine if you have passed the last element or just found empty/invalid elements. You must use the LAST method to determine the end of the collection.

```
If auth.exist(23) then …
```

The code fragment in the above example, checks for the existence of an element at position 23 before performing some operation.

EXTEND

Upon creation, the nested table and VARRAY collections start with no elements. To add an element, you must first make a location to place that element. This is the function of the EXTEND method. The EXTEND method without arguments will add one element to the collection. Used with arguments, the EXTEND method adds the defined number of elements and may initialize them

```
auth.extend;       -- creates space for one new element.
auth.extend(10);   -- creates space for 10 new elements.
auth.extend(10,0); -- creates space for 10 new elements.
                   -- Initialized the elements to 0.
```

The third line in the above example is used when the collection is defined as not null. In that case the extend method must create space and initialize the element.

The collection methods allow us to find move through a collection, test for valid elements and then process the data at that locations. At this point we are ready to introduce and use the three PL/SQL collections, starting with the VARRAY.

The PL/SQL VARRAY Collection

The VARRAY is one of the easier collections to understand and use, so that is where we will start. The VARRAY or variable array is a set of objects very much like a VARCHAR2 character string. A VARCHAR2 is defined with a maximum limit on the number of characters it can hold. A VARRAY is also defined with a maximum limit but instead of just holding characters, a VARRAY can hold any defined datatype. A VARRAY is a dense collection, meaning that you can only add or remove objects from the end. You define a VARRAY first as a type, and then define a variable that is the actual collection.

```
declare
  type auth_var is varray(1000) of author%rowtype;
  type authname_var is varray(300) of
                       author.auth_last_name%type;

  a_auth auth_var;
  a_aname authname_var;
begin …
```

If the VARRAYs and/or nested tables are stored as columns in the database, you must make the declaration persistent by declaring the type as a database object, shown in the next example.

```
create or replace type book_title_var as
    varray(20) of book.book_key%type;
```

Once the VARRAY is defined, elements can easily be inserted into the VARRAY.

```
SQL> declare
  2     type auth_var is varray(10) of
  3                        author.author_last_name%type;
  4     a_auth auth_var := auth_var();
  5  begin
  6     a_auth.extend;
  7     a_auth(1) := 'Smith';
  8     a_auth.extend;
  9     a_auth(2) := 'Jones';
 10     dbms_output.put_line(
                  a_auth(1) ||' and '|| a_auth(2));
 11  end; /

Smith and Jones
```

Lines 2 and 3 define the VARRAY type with a maximum of 10 elements. Line 4 defines the variable *a_auth* of *auth_var* type and it also initializes the array. A VARRAY can not be used until it is initialized. In line 4 the *auth_var()* function actually does the initialization.

Once the array is initialized you can extend it and add elements, which we do in lines 6 through 9. We access each element using the VARRAY variable and the index number. When the PL/SQL block ends (or the array variable goes out of scope), the memory used by the array is recovered automatically by the PL/SQL engine. Unlike a cursor, you do not close a collection.

A cursor can also be used to load the VARRAY. In this case you need to ensure that you do not exceed the array size.

```
SQL> declare
  2    type auth_var is varray(20) of
  3                         author.author_last_name%type;
  4    a_auth auth_var := auth_var();
  5  begin
  6    for r_c1 in
              (select author_last_name from author) loop
  7      a_auth(a_auth.last+1) := r_c1.author_last_name;
  8    end loop;
  9  end;
 10  /
declare
*
ERROR at line 1:
ORA-06502: PL/SQL: numeric or value error: NULL index
    table key value
ORA-06512: at line 7
```

Oops, it appears that we forgot that *a_auth.last* does not exist until we have at least one element. If the cursor is rewritten to first extend the array before loading the value we will not have this problem. In the example shown below, we load the array after checking for the array boundary.

```
SQL> declare
  2    type auth_var is varray(20) of
  3                         author.author_last_name%type;
  4    a_auth auth_var := auth_var();
  5    indx   number := 1;
  6  begin
  7    for r_c1 in
              (select author_last_name from author) loop
  8      if indx < a_auth.limit then
  9        a_auth.extend;
 10        a_auth(a_auth.last) := r_c1.author_last_name;
 11        dbms_output.put_line(a_auth(indx));
 12        indx := indx +1;
 13      end if;
 14    end loop;
 15  end;
 16  /

jones
hester
weaton
jeckle
withers
petty
clark
mee
shagger
smith
```

So what makes this collection so great? The next example is rather simple but it demonstrates the ability to perform multiple tasks on the collection. The listing is a bit long and is in the code depot under VARRAY.

First let's create an "included function" that returns the array. The function creates an array of *sales* table row types that match the passed *book_key* and returns the VARRAY. The included function is contained in lines 6 through 23.

```
SQL> declare
  2     type sales_array is varray(1000) of sales%rowtype;
  3     a_sal sales_array;
  4     n_avg number := 0;
  5
  6     function get_array (b_key in sales.book_key%type)
  7                         return sales_array
  8     as
  9     a_sales sales_array := sales_array();
 10     indx number := 1;
 11     cursor c1(v_key varchar2) is
 12      select * from sales where book_key = v_key
 13      order by order_number;
 14     begin
 15       for r_c1 in c1(b_key) loop
 16         if indx < a_sales.limit then
 17           a_sales.extend;
 18           a_sales(a_sales.last) := r_c1;
 19           indx := indx +1;
 20         end if;
 21       end loop;
 22       return a_sales;
 23     end;   -- function
```

Please note that line 2 and 3 define the VARRAY and the array variable, and notice that line 3 does not initialize the array. Instead, the function creates an array called *s_sales* and initializes it on line 9. The function used the same technique to load the array as the previous example. The VARRAY is returned to the calling procedure in line 22. Now we can simply call the function to get a fully loaded array, as shown below:

```
25  begin
26    for r_c2 in (select distinct book_key from sales
27                  order by book_key) loop
28      a_sal := get_array(r_c2.book_key);
29      --number of orders
30      dbms_output.put_line(
31        'Orders for Key '||r_c2.book_key||
                                ': '||a_sal.count);
32      --total sales
33      for  indx in a_sal.first..a_sal.last loop
34        n_avg := n_avg + a_sal(indx).quantity;
35      end loop;
36      n_avg := n_avg/a_sal.count;
37      dbms_output.put_line(
38        'Average Sales are
         '||to_char(n_avg,99999.00));
39      -- the third order for that book
40      dbms_output.put_line(
41        'The third order is
          '||a_sal(3).order_number);
42      -- the prior and next order
43      dbms_output.put_line(
44        'The second order is
              '||a_sal(a_sal.prior(3)).order_number);
45      dbms_output.put_line(
46        'The fourth order is
          '||a_sal(a_sal.next(3)).order_number);
47    end loop;
48  end;
49  /
```

Line 28 calls the function which first creates and then passes back the loaded VARRAY for each book_key in the cursor loop. Next a number of operations are performed on elements in the VARRAY.

Lines 33 through 35 of the above listing are very important because they demonstrate using a FOR loop along with the FIRST and LAST methods to efficiently move through the collection, one element at a time. What makes this very efficient is that the FOR loop will take care of checking that each element is valid.

If the loop finds a deleted element (which is not possible in a VARRAY) it will skip it and move to the next valid element. The example above performs four operations on each VARRAY.

Compared to using a cursor to retrieve the data for each operation from the database, the VARRAY is much more efficient. A partial example of the output is provided below.

```
Orders for Key B101: 5
Average Sales are   3640
The third order is O168
The second order is O129
The fourth order is O196
Orders for Key B102: 11
Average Sales are   1812
The third order is O104
The second order is O103
The fourth order is O105
Orders for Key B103: 9
```

Remember, a VARRAY is a collection of elements (all of which are the same data type). Elements can be added to the end of the VARRAY as long as the array limit set in the definition is not exceeded. You can not delete elements except at the end of a VARRAY.

```
SQL> declare
  2    type auth_var is varray(20) of
  3                           author.author_last_name%type;
  4    a_auth auth_var := auth_var();
  5    indx    number := 1;
  6  begin
  7    for r_c1 in
         (select author_last_name from author) loop
  8      if indx < a_auth.limit then
  9        a_auth.extend;
 10        a_auth(a_auth.last) := r_c1.author_last_name;
 11        indx := indx +1;
 12      end if;
 13    end loop;
 14    dbms_output.put_line(a_auth.count);
 15    a_auth.trim(5);
 16    dbms_output.put_line(a_auth.count);
 17    a_auth.delete;
 18    dbms_output.put_line(a_auth.count);
 19  end; /

10
5
0
```

Notice from the output that line 15 removed the last 5 elements while line 17 removed all the elements. If we attempt to delete the fifth element we get an error because you can only add or delete from the end of the VARRAY.

```
14    dbms_output.put_line(a_auth.count);
15    a_auth.delete(5);
16    dbms_output.put_line(a_auth.count);
17  end;
18  /

  a_auth.delete(5);
  *
ERROR at line 15:
ORA-06550: line 15, column 3:
PLS-00306: wrong number or types of arguments in call to 'DELETE'
ORA-06550: line 15, column 3:
PL/SQL: Statement ignored
```

A nested table is similar to a VARRAY except that it is a sparse collection, meaning that it can have deleted elements contained in the collection.

PL/SQL NESTED Tables

A "nested" table can be thought of as a single-column table that can either be in memory, or as a column in a database table. A nested table is very similar to a VARRAY except that the order of the elements is not static. Elements can be deleted or added anywhere in the nested table where as a VARRAY can only add or delete elements from the end of the array. Because a nested table can contain empty elements, it is know as a sparse collection. Nested tables can be declared in the PL/SQL block or in the database. If the nested table will be used in the database, the type definition must be in the database as shown below.

```
create or replace type auth_table as
                table of author.author_key%type;

type number_tab as table of number;
```

Notice that no boundary is defined for a nested table. A nested table has no set bounds other than the memory available to the database user.

As with a VARRAY, the nested table must also be initialized.

```
numb_list  number_tab := number_tab();
numb_list2 number_tab := number_tab(23,56,34,890,21);
```

The first line of the above example initializes an empty table while the second line initializes the table and loads the listed numbers into the table. Once initialized, the nested table is manipulated in the same manner as the VARRAY.

```
SQL> declare
  2    type number_tab is table of number;
  3    numb_list number_tab := number_tab(23,56,34,890,21);
  4  begin
  5    for indx in numb_list.first..numb_list.last loop
  6      dbms_output.put_line(numb_list(indx));
  7    end loop;
  8    numb_list.delete(2);
  9    numb_list.delete(4);
 10    for indx in numb_list.first..numb_list.last loop
 11      dbms_output.put_line(numb_list(indx));
 12    end loop;
 13  end;
 14  /

23
56
34
890
21
23

declare
*
ERROR at line 1:
ORA-01403: no data found
ORA-06512: at line 11
```

Using a sparse collection is causing us a few problems during execution as shown by the "no data found" error message. In the example above, the first FOR loop demonstrates retrieving the values in the nested table. In lines 8 and 9, elements inside the nested table are deleted, as opposed to deleting them from the end. When the second loop is attempted, an exception is raised when the code uses the second value. Remember that the DELETE method removes the element at that location but leaves the space. With a sparse collection, the existence of an element at each location must be checked. Below is the same example, except that the second loop verifies that the location contains an object.

```
SQL> declare
  2    type number_tab is table of number;
  3    numb_list number_tab := number_tab(23,56,34,890,21);
  4  begin
  5    for indx in numb_list.first..numb_list.last loop
  6      dbms_output.put_line(numb_list(indx));
  7    end loop;
  8    numb_list.delete(2);
  9    numb_list.delete(4);
 10    for indx in numb_list.first..numb_list.last loop
 11      if numb_list.exists(indx) then
 12        dbms_output.put_line(numb_list(indx));
 13      end if;
 14    end loop;
 15  end;
 16  /

23
56
34
890
21
23
34
21
```

One reason to implement nested tables in your code is the ability to load the entire nested table into the database as column values. This is a powerful feature but if you only need the collection in your PL/SQL code, you can skip some of the overhead imposed by nested tables and VARRAYs but using the memory only collection called PL/SQL tables.

PL/SQL Tables

As of Oracle9i PL/SQL tables were officially named ASSOCIATIVE ARRAYS. Most developers call associative arrays PL/SQL tables because they can not exist in the database, only in PL/SQL memory structures. The advantage over nested tables and VARRAYs is that a PL/SQL table does not have to be extended to add elements, nor does it have to be initialized. Best of all, elements are added in any order, in any position in the table.

PL/SQL tables before Oracle9i could only be indexed by BINARY_INTEGER, but from Oracle9i and beyond they can be indexed either by BINARY_INTEGER or a string type. You can conceptualize a PL/SQL table as a two-column table, the first being the index and the second being the data element. Like the other collection types, the index value is used to locate the data element.

In the example below, a PL/SQL table is defined and a cursor is used to load the collection and then read the elements out of the collection:

```
SQL> declare
  2    type book_tab is table of book.book_title%type
  3        index by binary_integer;
  4    book_list book_tab;
  5    indx      number := 1;
  6  begin
  7    for r_c3 in (select book_title from book) loop
  8      book_list(indx) := r_c3.book_title;
  9      indx := indx + 5;
 10    end loop;
 11    for xndx in book_list.first..book_list.last loop
 12      if book_list.exists(xndx) then
 13        dbms_output.put_line(book_list(xndx));
 14      end if;
 15    end loop;
 16  end;
 17  /
```

```
windows success
piano greats
   ...
cooking light
never eat meat
how to housebreak your horse
```

There is a lot to see in the example above. In line 3 the PL/SQL TABLE is defined as being INDEXED BY BINARY_INTEGER. In line 4 a variable was defined as the collection, but the collection was not initialized. Next, a cursor is used to load the current book titles into the collection, and the indexed value was increased by 5 each time a value was added.

Remember that the elements can be added in any order, any place in the collection. We see that line 11 initializes a FOR loop to access each value, and the FOR loop will go to each element space that is defined in the collection. Since this is a sparse collection (values can be deleted) element existence must be tested before accessing an element, and this test is performed on line 12. The example demonstrates that the PL/SQL Table is very similar to the nested table except that it does not have to be initialized, or extended.

Sometimes your data is paired with a string rather than a number and a data element is more efficiently accessed using the string. In the PUBS database, the *sales* table lists order numbers and the quantity sold. The order numbers are actually character strings. A PL/SQL TABLE can be created to allow access to the *quantity* values using the *order_number*. Since *order_number* is a varchar2 you will create the PL/SQL Table using the INDEX BY string method.

```
SQL> declare
  2    type orders_tab is table of number
  3          index by varchar2(20);
  4    orders_list orders_tab;
  5  begin
  6    for r_c4 in (select order_number,
  7                        quantity from sales) loop
```

```
 8       orders_list(r_c4.order_number) := r_c4.quantity;
 9    end loop;
10    dbms_output.put_line(orders_list('O102'));
11    dbms_output.put_line(orders_list('O109'));
12    dbms_output.put_line(orders_list('O193'));
13    dbms_output.put_line(orders_list('O156'));
14  end;
15  /

10
1020
5000
100
```

In the example above the collection is indexed by a string that will be the *order_number*. Line 3 defines this string index. Notice that you can not use a %TYPE in this definition. Line 8 loads the *quantity* values in the element defined by the *order_number*. The *order_number* is the index for the collection. In lines 10 through 13, the elements (*quantity*) stored at specified locations (*order_number*) are printed with *dbms_output.put_line*.

As we have noted, PL/SQL collections provide the developer with powerful tools to hold and process large data sets in memory, allowing data to be pulled from the database once, and used repeatedly as needed. If a developer needs to retrieve large numbers of rows from the database, it can be much more efficient to use a collection with a cursor and "bulk collect" the data in one operation.

The PL/SQL Bulk Collect Operation

As a DBA I tend to bulk collect everything…..even pizza.

Normally a developer will use a cursor to retrieve and process multiple rows of data, one at a time, but there are performance problems when dealing with large numbers of rows using cursors. As we have seen, a cursor fetches one row at a time, holding a consistent view, until all rows have been retrieved or the cursor is closed.

A performance issue arises from the fact that there are two engines in the database, the PL/SQL engine and the SQL engine. In some versions of the database, these engines actually have different capabilities resulting in some features being available in SQL but not in PL/SQL. When a cursor fetches a row of data it performs a "context switch" to the SQL engine, and it is the SQL component that retrieves the data. The SQL engine places the data in-memory and another context switch places us back into the PL/SQL engine.

The PL/SQL engine then continues processing until the next row is required, and the process repeats. A context switch is very fast, but if performed over and over again, the constant switching can take a noticeable amount of time. A bulk collect is a method of fetching data where the PL/SQL engine tells the SQL engine to collect many rows at once and place them in a collection. The SQL engine retrieves all the rows and loads them into the collection and switches back to the PL/SQL engine. All the rows are retrieved with only 2 context switches. The larger the number of rows processed, the more performance is gained by using a bulk collect.

In the Oracle10g database, the PL/SQL engine may perform a bulk collect for you. In 10g, a cursor loop may cause the PL/SQL engine to automatically bulk collect 100 rows at a time, allowing your code to process rows without having to setup and execute the bulk collect operation. As a result of this performance enhancement in 10g, bulk collecting 75 rows may not provide you with much of a benefit, while bulk collecting large numbers of rows (many hundreds) will still provide you with increased performance.

Bulk collecting data is easy. First, we define the collection or collections that will be used in the bulk collect. Next, define the cursor to retrieve the data and finally, bulk collect the data into the collections. The example below demonstrates a simple bulk collect:

```
SQL> declare
  2    type number_array is varray(10000) of
                                     number;
  3    type string_array is varray(10000) of
                                   varchar2(100);
  4
  5    a_store string_array;
  6    a_qty   number_array;
  7
  8    cursor c1 is
  9      select store_key, sum(quantity) from sales
 10      group by store_key;
 11  begin
 12    open c1;
 13      fetch c1 bulk collect into a_store, a_qty;
```

```
14     close c1;
15     for indx in a_store.first..a_store.last loop
16       dbms_output.put_line(
17             a_store(indx)||'....'||a_qty(indx));
18     end loop;
19   end; /

S102....21860
S105....13000
S109....12120
S101....2180
S106....6080
S103....7900
S104....13700
S107....24700
S108....5400
S110....3610
```

There is nothing new in the above example except line 13. Here instead of fetching one row, we bulk collect all the rows at once. Notice that this also allowed us to close the cursor and free the database resources it had obtained immediately after collecting the rows. The data can now be processed as needed in memory. In this example, lines 16 and 17 print out the data from the in-memory collection.

Also, note that the last example also used two arrays. The arrays were loaded together in the one BULK COLLECT INTO statement. As the SQL engine loaded the arrays, it places the data at the same index location in each array. If a store key existed in the table with no orders (not the case in this example), the store key would be place in the *a_store* array and a null would be placed in the *a_qty* array. This allows you to search the store array and retrieve the qty using the store array index. This is demonstrated in lines 15 through 18 in the example.

In database versions 9iR2 and later, you can bulk collect into records:

```
SQL> declare
  2    type sales_tab is table of sales%rowtype;
  3    t_sal sales_tab;
  4  begin
  5    select * bulk collect into t_sal from sales;
  6    dbms_output.put_line(t_sal.count);
  7  end;
  8  /

100
```

While a bulk collect retrieves data in bulk, the bulk load will change data in bulk.

The PL/SQL Bulk Load Operator

While bulk collect retrieves all the requested data from the database with two context switches, the bulk load will bulk manipulate the data in the same manner. The term bulk load does not really describe this capability; a better name would be bulk change. You can bulk update, delete, or insert. Bulk loading uses the FORALL clause to tell the SQL engine to execute the command on all rows meeting the specification. Although the FORALL clause looks like is FOR loop, it is different, primarily because there is no LOOP or END LOOP in the statement.

The example below selects over 12,000 object names and object ids from the database and then insert them into a table named *big_one*. First create the table to hold the data.

```
SQL> create table big_one as
  2    select object_name, object_id from dba_objects
  3    where 2 = 1;

Table created.
```

Now, bulk collect all the object names and ID numbers from the *dba_objects* view and then bulk load then into the *big_one* table. If you are not logged on as a user with DBA privilages the *dba_objects* view will not be available. In this case use the *user_objects* view, which contains fewer objects.

```
SQL> set timing on
SQL> declare
  2     type name_tab is table of
                  dba_objects.object_name%type;
  3     type id_tab   is table of
                  dba_objects.object_id%type;
  4     t_name name_tab;
  5     t_id   id_tab;
  6     cursor c1 is select object_name, object_id
  7                     from dba_objects;
  8  begin
  9     open c1;
 10     fetch c1 bulk collect into t_name, t_id;
 11     close c1;
 12     -- bulk insert
 13     forall indx in t_name.first..t_name.last
 14       insert into big_one values
 15           ( t_name(indx), t_id(indx));
 16  end;
 17  /


Elapsed: 00:00:00.00
SQL> select count(*) from big_one;

  COUNT (*)
----------
    12062
```

Wow, this process read and inserted over 12,000 rows in so little time that it did not even register on the timer. Notice that line 13 through 15 is actually one line of code. The FORALL clause passes the nested table collections to the SQL engine, which loads the data into the tables and then returns to the PL/SQL engine. These changes have not yet been committed and can still be rolled back if necessary.

The FORALL can also delete or update rows. Here we create a very large table by joining the *dba_objects* view and the *sales* table using a Cartesian product.

```
SQL> create table bigger_one as
  2     select book_key, quantity, object_id
  3     from dba_objects cross join sales;
Table created.

SQL> select count(*) from bigger_one;
```

```
  COUNT (*)
----------
  1206300
```

The *bigger_one* table has over a million rows. We want to increase the *quantity* value by 10 for all rows with *book_key* equals B103, B112, and B114. Finally we want to delete all the rows where the *book_key* equals B116, B106, and B109.

```
SQL> declare
  2     type book_tab is table of
                           sales.book_key%type;
  3
  4     t_book_add book_tab :=
                  book_tab('B103','B112','B114');
  5     t_book_del book_tab :=
                  book_tab('B116','B106','B109');
  6  begin
  7     forall indx in
                  t_book_add.first..t_book_add.last
  8       update bigger_one
                      set quantity = quantity + 10
  9        where book_key = t_book_add(indx);
 10     forall indx in
                  t_book_del.first..t_book_del.last
 11       delete from bigger_one
 12        where book_key = t_book_del(indx);
 13  end;
 14  /

Elapsed: 00:01:46.06
```

Even using bulk loads, the PL/SQL block took almost 2 minutes to complete. Lines 4 and 5 defined the collection variables and instantiated the nested tables. Lines 7 through 12 performed the actual work with two bulk loads. Do not forget that the changes are not permanent until a commit is issued.

A number of the examples provided so far have used included functions. Local functions are defined in the DECLARE section of the block. These functions were required because they used some defined variable or type from the outer block. There is a better way to share data and definitions within an application and that is by using PACKAGES.

Using PL/SQL Packages

A PL/SQL package is a grouping of related procedures, functions, definitions, and cursors. PL/SQL packages have these characteristics:

- The code placed in a package can see and use the other code inside the package.

- A cursor, variable, or type definition can be defined once and used anywhere in the package.

- Like the ADA programming language, PL/SQL packages have a specification and a body declaration.

- The code objects, definitions, procedures and functions defined in the package specification are accessible from outside the package.

- The code objects defined in the package body, but not in the specification, can not be seen or accessed outside the package. This allows a developer to hide code that he does not want the user to see.

A PL/SQL packages specification follows the format shown in the example below.

```
SQL> create or replace package myapp is
  2    procedure update_book_date
  3      (v_book_key in book.book_key%type,
  4       v_pub_date in book.book_date_published%type);
  5    function get_author
  6      (v_book_key in book.book_key%type)
                              return varchar2;
  7  end myapp;
  8  /

Package created.
```

The example specification above defines a package called *myapp* that contains one procedure and one function. Notice that the procedure and function body are not included. Only the name and passed parameters (or the signature) is included in the specification. The specification defines what is included the package that is exposed for use outside the package. To call a package object, include the package name using the dot (.) notation.

```
begin
  myapp.update_book_date('B101',SYSDATE);
  -- all the other suff
```

So where is the code for *myapp*'s objects? The code is in the package body, which is a separate database object. Any code object in the package specification is accessible from outside of the package. Any additional code objects defined in the package body (but not in the specification) are hidden and are not accessable from outside the package. Any code object in the package body can access any other code object in the package body.

In the example below, the procedure and function specified in the previous example is defined on lines 9 through 28.

```
SQL> create or replace package body myapp is
  2
  3     type number_var is varray(1000) of number;
  4
  5     cursor c1 is
  6       select order_number,quantity
  7       from sales;
  8
  9     procedure update_book_date
 10       (v_book_key in book.book_key%type,
 11        v_pub_date in
                       book.book_date_published%type)
 12     is
 13     begin
 14       update book
 15         set book_date_published = v_pub_date
 16         where book_key = v_book_key;
 17     end;
 18
 19     function get_author
 20       (v_book_key in book.book_key%type)
           return varchar2
 21     is
```

```
22      auth_store author.author_last_name%type;
23    begin
24      select author_last_name into auth_store
25      from author join book_author
          using (author_key)
26      where book_key = v_book_key;
27      return auth_store;
28    end;
29
30  end myapp;
31  /
```

```
Package body created.
```

Notice that the example defines a VARRAY type on line 3 and a
cursor on line 5. These objects can be used anywhere in the
package but can not be accessed outside the package. Since code
objects defined in the package can be shared, you do not have to
redefine them when used. Here is a partial listing of the package
body for the example package specification.

The entire listing is in the code depot.

```
SQL> create or replace package body myapp is
  2
  3      type number_var is varray(1000) of number;
  4      type string_var is varray(1000)
                                    of varchar2(80);
  5
  6      cursor c1(v_key varchar2) is
  7        select order_number,quantity
  8        from sales where store_key = v_key;
  9
 10
 11      function get_average_sales
 12        (v_store_key in varchar2) return number
 13      is
 14        a_order string_var;
 15        a_qty   number_var;
 16        n_avg   number;
 17      begin
 18        open c1(v_store_key);
 19        fetch c1 bulk collect into a_order, a_qty;
 20        for indx in
            a_order.first..a_order.last loop
 21          n_avg := n_avg + a_qty(indx);
 22        end loop;
 23        return n_avg/a_order.count;
 24      end;
 25
procedure update_book_date
…   -- code continues
```

Two VARRAYs are defined on lines 3 and 4 and they are used in the function defined on lines 14 and 15. The function does not have to redefine the types. The cursor defined on line 6 is again used on line 18 without having to redefine it inside the function.

We have been using packages throughout this book, mostly the *dbms_output* package supplied by Oracle. We have made extensive use of the *put_line* procedure inside of that package, but that is not the only procedure in the package.

But how do you determine the code objects that a package exposes in the package specification? Just like a database table, you describe it:

```
SQL> desc dbms_output

PROCEDURE DISABLE

PROCEDURE ENABLE
 Argument Name                     Type                    In/Out Default?
 --------------------------------  ----------------------  ------ --------
 BUFFER_SIZE                       NUMBER(38)              IN     DEFAULT

PROCEDURE GET_LINE
 Argument Name                     Type                    In/Out Default?
 --------------------------------  ----------------------  ------ --------
 LINE                              VARCHAR2                OUT
 STATUS                            NUMBER(38)              OUT

PROCEDURE GET_LINES
 Argument Name                     Type                    In/Out Default?
 --------------------------------  ----------------------  ------ --------
 LINES                             TABLE OF VARCHAR2(32767) OUT
 NUMLINES                          NUMBER(38)              IN/OUT

PROCEDURE GET_LINES
 Argument Name                     Type                    In/Out Default?
 --------------------------------  ----------------------  ------ --------
 LINES                             DBMSOUTPUT_LINESARRAY   OUT
 NUMLINES                          NUMBER(38)              IN/OUT

PROCEDURE NEW_LINE

PROCEDURE PUT
 Argument Name                     Type                    In/Out Default?
 --------------------------------  ----------------------  ------ --------
 A                                 VARCHAR2                IN

PROCEDURE PUT_LINE
 Argument Name                     Type                    In/Out Default?
 --------------------------------  ----------------------  ------ --------
 A                                 VARCHAR2                IN
```

There are eight procedures in the *dbms_output* package. Notice that three of the procedures have the same name. This is called overloading and in PL/SQL can only exist in a package. Outside of a package a procedure or function is defined by a name. No two objects can have the same name. But inside a package, objects are defined by their signature, which consist of the name and the passed parameters.

If you look closely at the three *get_lines* procedures you will see that each one requires a different number and/or type of parameters. Thus, the three procedure names are the same but the three signatures are distinct. In the *myapp* package defined in the previous example, there is a function that returns the author's last name when passed a *book_key* (the author of the book). This same function can be used if passed an *author_key*. To overload the function, simply define the new function passing the new variables as in the partial listing below.

```
36    function get_author
37      (v_book_key in book.book_key%type)
   return varchar2
38    is
39      auth_store author.author_last_name%type;
40    begin
41      select author_last_name into auth_store
42      from author join book_author
         using (author_key)
43      where book_key = v_book_key;
44      return auth_store;
45    end;
46
47    function get_author
48      (v_auth_key in author.author_key%type)
         return varchar2
49    is
50      auth_store author.author_last_name%type;
51    begin
52      select author_last_name into auth_store
53      from author
54      where author_key = v_auth_key;
55      return auth_store;
56    end;
57  end myapp;
58  /

Package body created.
```

The function *get_author* is now overloaded inside the *myapp* package. Before anyone can access the overloaded function, it must be added to the specification.

```
SQL> create or replace package myapp is
  2     procedure update_book_date
  3        (v_book_key in book.book_key%type,
  4         v_pub_date in
                    book.book_date_published%type);
  5     function get_author
  6        (v_book_key in book.book_key%type)
           return varchar2;
  7     function get_author
  8        (v_auth_key in author.author_key%type)
            return varchar2;
 10  end myapp;
 11  /
```

The new function can now be accessed from outside the package. When packages are used, it is important to use descriptive names for passed parameters. When the package is described, these names are exposed.

```
SQL> desc myapp

FUNCTION GET_AUTHOR RETURNS VARCHAR2
 Argument Name                     Type                     In/Out Default?
 ------------------------------    ----------------------   ------ --------
 V_BOOK_KEY                        VARCHAR2(6)              IN

FUNCTION GET_AUTHOR RETURNS VARCHAR2
 Argument Name                     Type                     In/Out Default?
 ------------------------------    ----------------------   ------ --------
 V_AUTH_KEY                        VARCHAR2(11)             IN

PROCEDURE UPDATE_BOOK_DATE
 Argument Name                     Type                     In/Out Default?
 ------------------------------    ----------------------   ------ --------
 V_BOOK_KEY                        VARCHAR2(6)              IN
 V_PUB_DATE                        DATE                     IN
```

Many times the example above is all a user who is attempting to use this package will see. A descriptive parameter name is important in helping the user know what variable to pass as a parameter. Notice that the *%type* parameter datatypes are displayed as the actual variable's datatype (varchar2(x) in this example), so the name becomes important in displaying to the programmer the makeup of the parameters.

So, when should you use packages? Always! You should write the application code in packages. Small applications can be placed in a single package. It is easier to write the code in a package than to write and test it as a stand alone object and then move it into a package. Code written outside of packages and then moved into packages rarely takes advantage of the package's code, definition sharing, and overloading. Also, each object will have to be tested and validated again once it is in the package.

Using packages will also allow the database to more efficiently process the code. When the first code object in a package is called, the database loads the entire package into memory. So by placing the application into packages, the code will be loaded and maintained in memory, resulting in faster execution and more efficient use of the database resources. In fact, the DBA can pin the package into the library cache on database startup so that it is loaded even before the first user logs on.

Dynamic SQL in PL/SQL

The programmer actually has two methods for executing a SQL statement within PL/SQL, the embedded method which we have been using throughout the book, and implementing dynamic SQL. There are many times when a SQL statement needs to be built and executed dynamically. When using SQL*Plus creating and executing dynamic SQL is a fairly simple task; create a script that generates the SQL, and then run the script. The script below will create the commands to truncate all the tables in the PUBS schema.

```
set pages 0 line 132 feedback off trim on
spool /opt/script/truncate.sql
select
  'truncate table '||tablename||';'
```

```
from user_tables;
spool off;
set pages 999 feedback on
@/opt/script/truncate.sql
```

In PL/SQL the SQL statement is created as a string, which is then executed using the EXECUTE IMMEDIATE clause.

```
SQL> declare
  2    v_str varchar2(200);
  3  begin
  4    for r_c1 in (select * from user_tables) loop
  5      v_str:= 'delete '||r_c1.table_name;
  6      dbms_output.put_line(v_str);
  7      execute immediate v_str;
  8    end loop;
  9  end;
 10  /

delete AUTHOR
delete EMP
delete JOB
delete PUBLISHER
delete SALES
delete STORE
delete BOOK_AUTHOR
delete BOOK

SQL> rollback
```

Notice that you still need to execute a commit to make the changes permanent. The ROLLBACK statement in the above example returns the deleted rows to the tables.

The EXECUTE IMMEDIATE clause allows the application to build different SQL statements based on user input or application errors. It also allows the developer to dynamically tune the application. A report may require a set of indexes to operate efficiently; however, these indexes may harm database performance if left in the database all the time. Using dynamic SQL, the application can build the indexes, run the report, and then delete the indexes upon completion.

```
SQL> begin
  2    execute immediate 'create index ln_idx
  3                  on author(author_last_name)';
```

```
   4    execute immediate 'create index fn_idx
   5                on author(author_first_name)';
   6    -- run_big_report;
   7    execute immediate 'drop index ln_idx';
   8    execute immediate 'drop index fn_idx';
   9  end;
  10  /
```

Dynamic SQL is easy to implement and very powerful. When creating database objects, such as shown in the example above, be careful that the cost of creating the object is not greater than the cost of running the report without the object.

There is one significant issue with using dynamic SQL. A dynamical SQL statement submitted to the database using EXECUTE IMMEDIATE does not use bind variables. SQL statements in PL/SQL blocks automatically use bind variables, but dynamic SQL cannot. Bind variables allow the database to reuse stored execution plans. Never use dynamic SQL when a normal SQL statement will work. If you want the details of how the database used bind variables, look through any Oracle database tuning book, they will cover it in detail.

Triggers

A trigger is a block of PL/SQL code that executes when a database event occurs. Because the database executes the trigger, no parameters can be passed in, or returned by, a trigger. The trigger can execute any PL/SQL code other PL/SQL block can execute, to include calling procedures and functions, DML or DDL (creating or manipulating objects or data).

If I can get this trigger to fire, I will sink their battleship!
These Navy guys are soooo easy!

Since a trigger executes on a database event, it can capture, change, or update data being inserted, updated, or deleted to include stopping undesirable changes. Triggers can be used to replicate data to other tables, insert data into tables with foreign key constraints in the correct order, or just about anything else you can do in PL/SQL.

Triggers execute on database events. In Oracle 8i and above, just about anything that happens in the database can have a trigger attached to it. This includes database startup/shutdown, user logon/logoff, and server errors. Triggers can also be attached to event against database objects such as tables.

There are two types of triggers on a table event: a statement level trigger and a row level trigger. A statement level trigger executes once when the event happens. If you are performing a bulk insert and want to log that an insert took place you would use a statement level trigger to add one log entry for the bulk insert (even though you may insert 1000 rows). A row level trigger executes for every row acted upon during the event. In a bulk insert, the row level trigger will execute for each row being inserted. The row level trigger contains the FOR ALL ROWS clause.

The example below is a statement level trigger.

```
create trigger
    t1
on insert or update or delete on
    book
begin
  myapp.log_event;
end;
```

On a bulk operation this trigger will execute once, no matter how many rows are inserted, updated, or deleted. The example below is basically the same trigger as a row level trigger.

```
create trigger
    t2
on insert or update or delete on
    book
for each row
begin
  myapp.log_event;
end;
```

This trigger will execute once for each row inserted, updated or deleted.

The specification for a trigger differs from the procedure or function in that it must tell the database on what event the trigger is executed and if the trigger executes before the event or after it. Some events are restricted in their execution capabilities. For example, a trigger that executes before the database startup event is not possible, nor is it possible to execute a trigger after a database shutdown event.

Let's look at using a trigger to create complicated primary keys for tables in the PUBS database. In the PUBS database the primary keys are a varchar2 datatype that is based on a sequence.

For the *author* table, the primary key starts with a letter 'A' followed by at least three numbers. What we need is a trigger that creates a new key for the *author* table when a row is inserted. The key is needed for each row so this will be a row level trigger.

First, we create a sequence for the trigger to use. Note that the sequence starts at the number 20 to account for the rows that are already in the table.

```
SQL> create sequence author_key_seq
  2   increment by 1
  3   start with 20
  4   cache 3 noorder
  5  /

Sequence created.
```

Now create a trigger on the author table that creates the new primary key when a row is inserted. The example below creates a row level trigger that executes before a row is inserted into the table. It generates the primary key and replaces the row's primary key column with the new key before the row is inserted into the table.

```
SQL> create or replace trigger author_key_gen_tr
  2   before insert on author
  3   for each row
  4   declare
  5     n_number number;
  6   begin
  7     select author_key_seq.nextval into n_number
          from dual;
  8     :NEW.author_key := 'A'||lpad(n_number,3,0);
  9   end;
 10  /

Trigger created.
```

There are a couple of new items in the example above. Line 2 defined the event that the trigger will fire on, before every insert on the author table. This trigger will not fire on updates or deletes. Line 3 specifies that the trigger will fire for each row inserted. The trigger will fire for every row, single insert or bulk insert. Line 8 introduces a new notation. The :OLD and :NEW notation are used to reference the row data before the trigger execution and after the trigger execution. Note that we are referencing the values before and after the trigger execution, not the event. In the example above, the trigger does not care what (if anything) is inserted in the *author_key* column. The trigger creates a new key from the sequence and places it in the *:new.author_key* variable, which is then inserted into the table instead of the column value before the trigger fired. The SQL in the example below inserts one row of data into the *author* table.

```
SQL> insert into author values
  2  ( ''
  3  , 'Spade'
  4  , 'Sam'
  5  , '234-234-5678'
  6  , '123 Here St'
  7  , 'Thereville'
  8  , 'ST'
  9  , '98765'
 10  , '45822');

1 row created.
```

Here a row is inserted into the *author* table with a blank (or NULL) *author_key* column. When the *author_key* is selected from the table, you can see that the trigger created a key value and placed it into the row before the row was inserted into the table.

```
SQL> select
  2     author_key
  3  from author
  4     where author_last_name = 'Spade';

AUTHOR_KEY
-----------
A020
```

Here is another example that maintains a history of changes to a table. Updates and deletes are copied to a history table using a trigger. This trigger takes advantage of the triggers ability to determine which event was executed. Using this capability, the trigger can execute different sections of code based on the even that executed. The three test conditions are INSERTING, UPDATING and DELETING. The test will be TRUE for the event that executed the trigger.

```
if (updating) then…
```

To see this capability in action, first create the *sales_history* table to hold the old rows from the *sales* table. This table will have the same columns as the *sales* table plus a column for the change date and a column for the change method.

```
SQL> CREATE TABLE SALES_HISTORY
  2  ( CHG_DATE          DATE
  3  , CHG_TYPE          VARCHAR2(6)
  4  , STORE_KEY         VARCHAR2(4)
  5  , BOOK_KEY          VARCHAR2(6)
  6  , ORDER_NUMBER      VARCHAR2(20)
  7  , ORDER_DATE        DATE
  8  , QUANTITY          NUMBER(5))
  9  /

Table created.
```

Now create a trigger that will capture the table changes and place the old data into the *sales_history* table.

```
SQL> create or replace trigger sales_history_tr
  2  before update or delete on sales
  3  for each row
  4  begin
  5    if (updating) then
  6      insert into sales_history
  7        ( CHG_DATE
  8        , CHG_TYPE
  9        , STORE_KEY
 10        , BOOK_KEY
 11        , ORDER_NUMBER
 12        , ORDER_DATE
 13        , QUANTITY)
 14      values
 15        ( sysdate
 16        , 'UPDATE'
 17        , :old.STORE_KEY
 18        , :old.BOOK_KEY
 19        , :old.ORDER_NUMBER
 20        , :old.ORDER_DATE
 21        , :old.QUANTITY);
 22    else
```

```
23        insert into sales_history
24          ( CHG_DATE
25          , CHG_TYPE
26          , STORE_KEY
27          , BOOK_KEY
28          , ORDER_NUMBER
29          , ORDER_DATE
30          , QUANTITY)
31        values
32          ( sysdate
33          , 'DELETE'
34          , :old.STORE_KEY
35          , :old.BOOK_KEY
36          , :old.ORDER_NUMBER
37          , :old.ORDER_DATE
38          , :old.QUANTITY);
39      end if;
40    end; /
```

The above example uses the :OLD specification to capture the
values in the row before it is changed and save them to the
sales_history table, along with the change date/time and the change
type (update or delete). Notice the condition test at line 5 to
determine if the event was an update or a delete.

Sometimes the :OLD and :NEW reference is confusing. You can
redefine these names using the referencing clause. The example
below replaces the standard notation with early and late

```
SQL> create or replace trigger sales_history2_tr
  2  before update or delete on sales
  3  referencing old as early new as late
  4  for each row
  5  begin
  6      insert into sales_history
  7        ( CHG_DATE,
  8        CHG_TYPE,
  9        STORE_KEY,
 10        BOOK_KEY,
 11        ORDER_NUMBER,
 12        ORDER_DATE,
 13        QUANTITY)
 14      values
 15        ( sysdate,
 16        'UPDATE',
 17        :early.STORE_KEY,
 18        :early.BOOK_KEY,
 19        :early.ORDER_NUMBER,
 20        :early.ORDER_DATE,
 21        :early.QUANTITY);
```

```
22  end;
23  /
```

Trigger created.

Often the default values are defined in the referencing clause for clarity.

```
create or replace trigger sales_history2_tr
before update or delete on sales
referencing old as old new as new
for each row
begin
  ...
```

A trigger does not need to perform an action on the object that fired the event. Below is a trigger that fires after an insert on a table and executes a procedure in a package.

```
SQL> create or replace trigger do_something_tr
  2   after insert on book_author
  3   begin
  4      ref_cursor_pak.sales_row_count;
  5   end;
  6   /
```

Trigger created.

This trigger executes the procedure *sales_row_count* from the *ref_cursor_pak* example after each insert into the *book_author* tables.

```
SQL> insert into book_author values
  2    ('A101','B110',.15);
Number of rows: 0
First Order Number: O101
First Order Number: O102
Number of rows: 2
Cursor Closed

1 row created.
```

In the example, it appears that the trigger fired before the row was created. That is not the case. The results appear that way because of the manner that SQL*Plus retrieved the results from the buffer. Because the trigger executes after the insert event, if the insert fails, the trigger will not fire.

```
SQL> insert into book_author values
  2     ('A101','B110');
insert into book_author values
            *
ERROR at line 1:
ORA-00947: not enough values
```

Notice that the trigger did not fire because the row insertion failed.

PL/SQL, Triggers, and Mutating Tables

A mutation table is defined as a table that is changing. But in dealing with triggers, it is a table that has the possibility of changing. What this means to a trigger is that if the trigger reads a table, it can not change the table that it read from. This does not impact the exclusive use of :OLD and :NEW. It says that if the trigger reads the table (such as using a SELECT query), that changes (even using :NEW) will fail. This can also happen when a trigger on a parent table causes an insert on a child table referencing a foreign key. The insert to the child table caused the foreign key to validate the data on the parent (which fired the trigger) causing the insert of the child table to result in a mutating table error on the parent table.

Each new release of the Oracle database reduces the impact of the mutating table error on triggers and they are much less of a problem with Oracle9i and above. If a trigger does result in a mutating table error, the only real option is to rewrite the trigger as a statement-level trigger. Mutating table errors only impact row level triggers. But to use a statement level trigger, some data may need to be preserved from each row, to be used by the statement level trigger. This data can be stored in a PL/SQL collection or in a temporary table. A simple row level trigger that causes a mutating table error can result in a very complicated statement level trigger to achieve the needed result.

Here are some important items to remember about triggers.

- On insert triggers have no :OLD values.

- On delete triggers have no :NEW values.

- Triggers do not commit transactions. If a transaction is rolled back, the data changed by the trigger is also rolled back.

- Commits, rollbacks and save points are not allowed in the trigger body. A commit/rollback affects the entire transaction, it is all or none.

- Unhandled exceptions in the trigger will cause a rollback of the entire transaction, not just the trigger.

- If more than one trigger is defined on an event, the order in which they fire is not defined. If the triggers must fire in order, you must create one trigger that executes all the actions in the required order.

- A trigger can cause other events to execute triggers.

- A trigger can not change a table that it has read from. This is the mutating table error issue.

The fact that a trigger can cause other triggers to fire is an important item to remember. A trigger that causes other database events to execute triggers can cause the database crash. For example, the database can capture server errors by defining a trigger on the database server error event.

But if this trigger causes a server error, the database will spin in a loop, with each firing of the trigger causing the error, firing the trigger again, and again, and again. The only way to regain control of the database is to disable the trigger.

Disabling/Enabling Triggers

Sometimes triggers cause problems and you need to turn them off temporarily. This is an easy procedure as shown in the example below.

```
alter trigger sales_history_tr disable;
alter trigger sales_history_tr enable;
```

A disabled trigger remains in the database but will not execute. To remove a trigger from the database, simply drop it.

```
drop trigger sales_history_tr;
```

Triggers are a powerful tool when used correctly. Triggers are the basis for many of the advanced capabilities built into the Oracle database such as multi-master replication and materialized views.

Conclusion

This chapter covered a lot of advanced PL/SQL topics from collections and bulk operation, to packages and triggers. A lot of these topics are advanced PL/SQL and their use is ignored by the casual PL/SQL developer. But as you have seen in this Chapter, many of these topics are powerful features that will make your PL/SQL program run more efficiently, both to the user and to the database.

Collections are used to store objects in memory. PL/SQL provides three types of collections: VARRAYs, Nested Tables, and PL/SQL Tables. The VARRAY and Nested Tables are database objects and can be place in database tables. VARRAYs and Nester Tables type definition can exist in the PL/SQL code or in the database. PL/SQL Tables exist only in memory. All three collections are homogeneous in that they can hold only one datatype such as a value, record or row type.

A VARRAY is an array of objects. It is a dense collection, so an object can only be added or removed at the end of the array. Nested Tables and PL/SQL tables are sparse collections meaning that data can be deleted from anywhere in the collection. PL/SQL tables are indexes by either BINARY_INTEGER or varchar2. The index provides the access to the object value.

Bulk Collects and Bulk Loads use the power of collections to perform data manipulation in groups. A bulk collect passes a query and one or more collections to the SQL engine, which retrieves the data and loads the collections.

In a bulk load, the SQL engine is passed a loaded collection and a SQL statement, and executes the statement against each value in the collection. Bulk collects and bulk loads are much more efficient that a single row fetch when dealing with large numbers of rows.

Packages are logical groups of PL/SQL code objects such as type definitions, cursors, procedures and functions. They facilitate data persistence, procedure and function overloading, and module design. Objects defined in the specification are public and can be called from outside of the package. Objects in the package body that are not in the specification are hidden and are only available to code inside the package.

Triggers are anonymous PL/SQL blocks that are executed when events happen in the database:

- Each trigger is tied to one event, but an event can have multiple triggers.

- The trigger can execute before or after the event.

- Triggers on tables can be row level triggers that fire for each row, or statement level triggers that fire once for each event.

- Triggers can not be passed parameters, nor can they return values.

- If an event has multiple triggers defined on it, the database does not guarantee the order the triggers will be executed.

- Triggers can also cause other triggers to fire.

You now have the skills to start effectively programming in PL/SQL. Hopefully you followed the examples in the book after loading the PUBS database. My intent was to provide you with as many examples of real world code that you can use as a reference as you build your own applications. Like all programming, you will get better by doing it, so keep up your skills.

Index

About John Garmany

John Garmany is a graduate of West Point, an Airborne Ranger and a retired Lt. Colonel with 20+ years of IT experience.

John is an OCP Certified Oracle DBA with a Master's Degree in Information Systems, a Graduate Certificate in Software Engineering, and a BS degree (Electrical Engineering) from West Point.

A respected Oracle expert and author, John serves as a writer for Oracle Internals, DBAZine and Builder.com. John is the author of "Logical Database Design - Principles & Practices" by CRC Press, the "Oracle9iAS Administration Handbook" by Oracle Press and "Oracle Replication - Snapshot, Multi-master & Materialized Views Scripts" and "Oracle SQL*Plus Reports - Fast reporting with SQL and SQL*Plus" by Rampant TechPress.

About Mike Reed

When he first started drawing, Mike Reed drew just to amuse himself. It wasn't long, though, before he knew he wanted to be an artist. Today he does illustrations for children's books, magazines, catalogs, and ads.

He also teaches illustration at the College of Visual Art in St. Paul, Minnesota. Mike Reed says, "Making pictures is like acting — you can paint yourself into the action." He often paints on the computer, but he also draws in pen and ink and paints in acrylics. He feels that learning to draw well is the key to being a successful artist.

Mike is regarded as one of the nation's premier illustrators and is the creator of the popular "Flame Warriors" illustrations at www.flamewarriors.com, a website devoted to Internet insults. "To enter his Flame Warriors site is sort of like entering a hellish Sesame Street populated by Oscar the Grouch and 83 of his relatives." – Los Angeles Times.
(http://redwing.hutman.net/%7Emreed/warriorshtm/lat.htm)

Mike Reed has always enjoyed reading. As a young child, he liked the Dr. Seuss books. Later, he started reading biographies and war stories. One reason why he feels lucky to be an illustrator is because he can listen to books on tape while he works. Mike is available to provide custom illustrations for all manner of publications at reasonable prices. Mike can be reached at www.mikereedillustration.com.